The Other Ten Wolves
A YELLOWSTONE BACKSTORY

CARTER NIEMEYER
First print edition 2025 Copyright © Bottlefly Press

THE OTHER TEN WOLVES
A YELLOWSTONE BACKSTORY

Published by Bottlefly Press
Boise, Idaho

Copyright © 2025 by Carter Niemeyer

All rights reserved, including the right of reproduction or electronic storage in whole or in part in any form.

Edited by Jenny Niemeyer and Linwood Laughy
Cover photo by Julie Argyle
Maps and graphics by Jenny Niemeyer

This is a work of non-fiction. All of the events actually happened. Some names and identifying details have been changed to protect the privacy of individuals. Nothing is intended or should be interpreted as expressing or representing the views of the United States Government or other government departments or agencies.

This book was produced by human beings.

First paperback edition 2025 ISBN 978735129808

Library of Congress CIP 2025902525
Nature—Animals—
—Autobiography/memoir

Also available in ebook and audiobook

For inquiries contact the publisher bottleflypressbooks@icloud.com

10 9 8 7 6 5 4 3 2 1

Also by Carter Niemeyer

Wolfer

Wolf Land

This book is dedicated to all of the advocates, scientists and citizens who worked together during the early years of wolf recovery in the West. We gave and got, and because we did, we succeeded. There will never be another time like it.

"To learn something new,
take the path that you took yesterday."

—John Burroughs (1837-1921)

Preface

The story of the Sawtooth wolves has not been told, at least not like this. I find this fact incredible, because a quarter of the wolves reintroduced to Yellowstone National Park were from a wild pack in Montana—the Sawtooth pack. The ten pups in this story were not part of the original reintroduction plan, and that is probably why their lives have been mostly forgotten.

By 2001, I'd been in the wolf management and control world for nearly twenty years, working mostly for a U.S. Department of Agriculture wildlife control agency called Wildlife Services. My last job, however, was with the U.S. Fish and Wildlife Service as the wolf recovery manager for Idaho. This was another all-consuming job, but mostly more of the same: saving wolves, moving them, killing them, until all the available habitat was full. I was a problem-solver, even if the solutions didn't make everyone—or anyone—happy. My job was thrilling and heartbreaking, even if I didn't fully realize it at the time. After I retired in 2006, people frequently asked me about this wolf or that wolf, and I realized I had a lot of stories to tell.

In 2022, I flew to Minneapolis for the International Wolf Conference. I always enjoy seeing old friends and talking shop. Our past adventures were starting to gather dust. We were not so much biologists now as historians. After dinner, I attended an evening session—a short film by renowned wildlife cinematographer Bob Landis. The film, titled *Three Wolves, Three Packs: Mother, Daughter, Grandmother*, was about a line of white wolves in Yellowstone, three of them at the time. Afterward, a panel featuring Doug Smith and wolf project biologists Dan Stahler, Jeremy SunderRaj and Kira Cassidy discussed the film.

I sat with my mouth open. Here, unfolding before me, was the story of the Sawtooth and Nez Perce packs' descendants. It was full of so much drama and so many soap-opera-worthy moments.

Today, the story stretches far beyond the Sawtooth and Nez Perce packs because that's how genetics carry on. But the origin of this tale has been lost, partly because there are few who remember it, and partly because it has been eclipsed by other noteworthy Yellowstone wolves. Even the physical remnants of reintroduction are disappearing. In 2000, park employees dismantled most of the wolf acclimation pens, but they left the one at Rose Creek. Over the years, falling trees have crushed some of its wire panels, but as long as even part of this pen remains, people will hike there to see where some of the Yellowstone wolf story began.

I went to my journals—a stack of them I'd kept since 1973. I'd already used my notes to write two memoirs, *Wolfer* and *Wolf Land*, and now I was turning to them again. I knew the Sawtooth wolves personally, and I wanted to write their story. In the past, whenever I mentioned the Sawtooth puppies, I was mostly met with blank looks. "Do you mean the captive Sawtooth wolves in Idaho that belonged to the Dutchers?" No, no. My Sawtooth wolves were wild wolves. I discovered that most people didn't know a thing about them.

While the Sawtooth experiment was happening in 1996, Yellowstone National Park officials were less than thrilled. It was true that the youngsters were tainted with the sins of their parents, who were livestock killers. But somehow it seemed the Sawtooth pups were held to a higher standard than all the other reintroduced wolves. Maybe all of the publicity surrounding the pups' captures caused them to be under a microscope in a way that other Yellowstone wolves were not. As it turned out, the Sawtooth experiment was no less successful than the rest of Yellowstone's reintroduction, though it wasn't trotted out as a success. Sometimes the pups weren't mentioned at all.

For me, the saga of the Sawtooth and Nez Perce packs happened up close and far away. When a wolf I captured was sent to Yellowstone, the animal generally fell out of my life because it was out of my jurisdiction. I knew very few of the park's wolves. Unless they got in trouble with livestock, our paths didn't cross. But when it came to the Sawtooth wolves, our paths *did* cross, and those memories are as fresh today as they were 30 years ago.

—Carter Niemeyer, Spring 2025

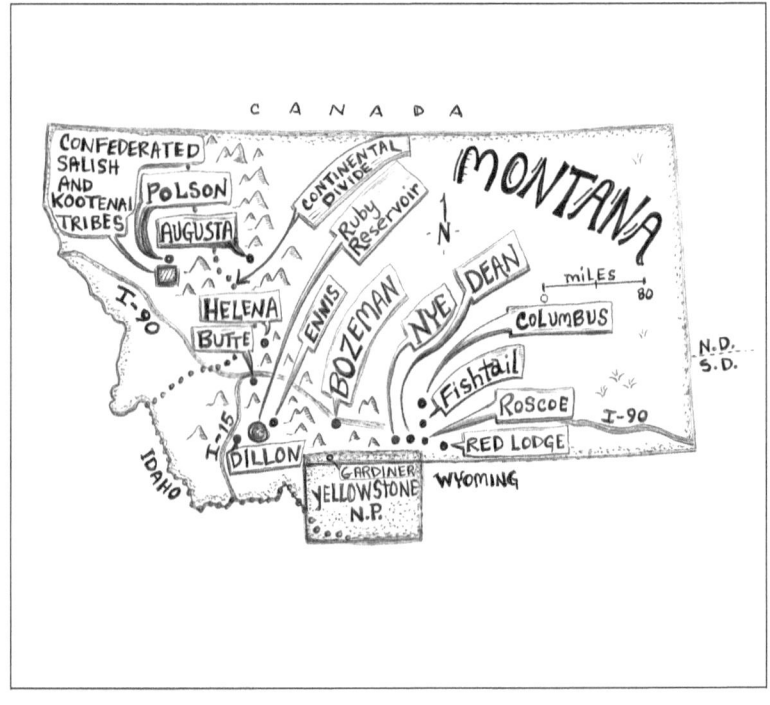

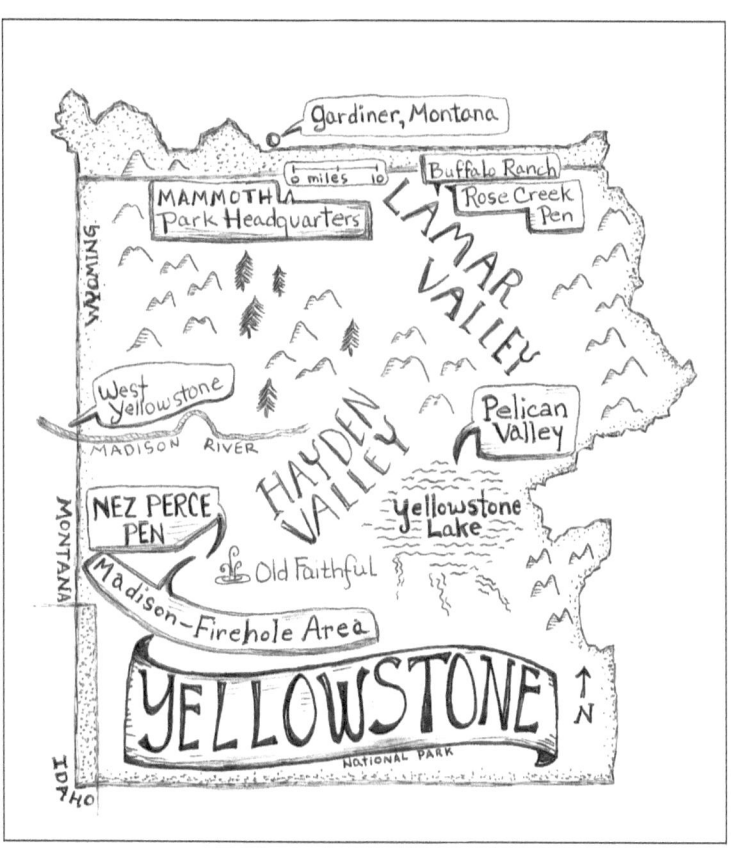

Sawtooth/Nez Perce Pack Family Tree

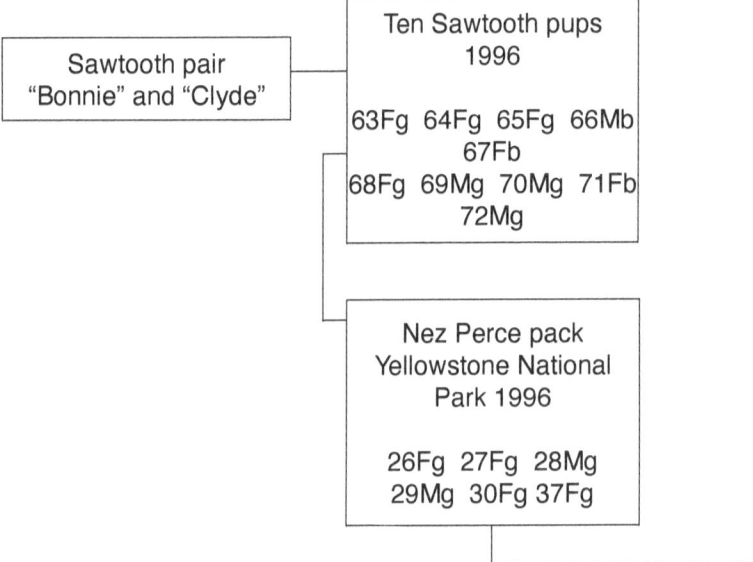

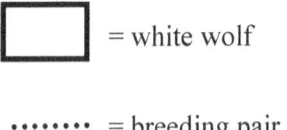 = white wolf

.... = breeding pair

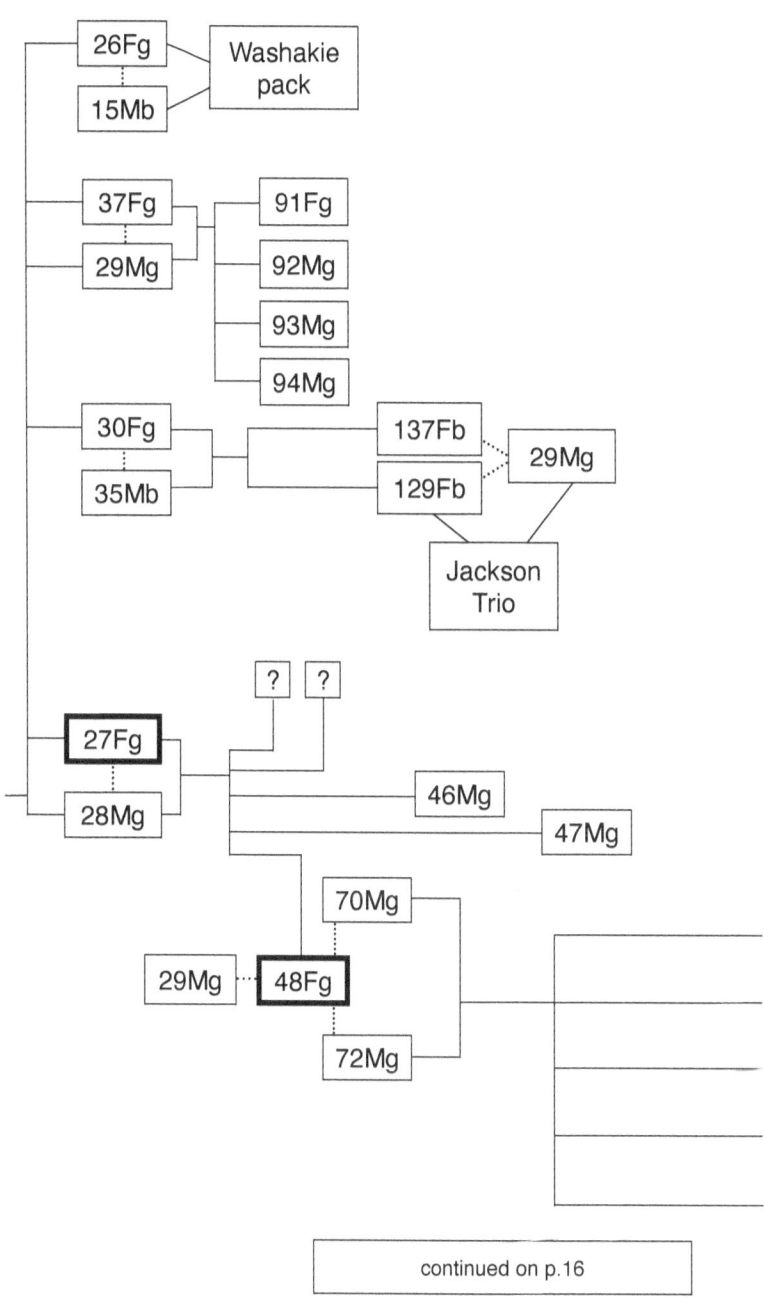

continued on p.16

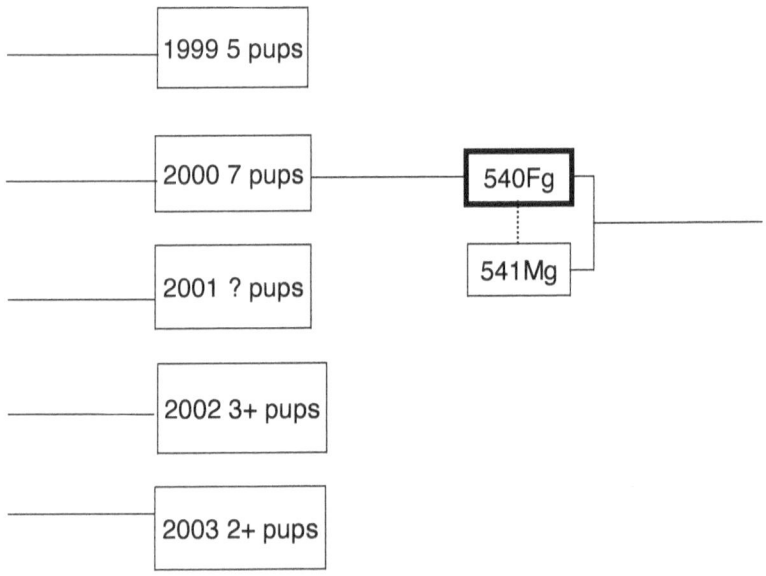

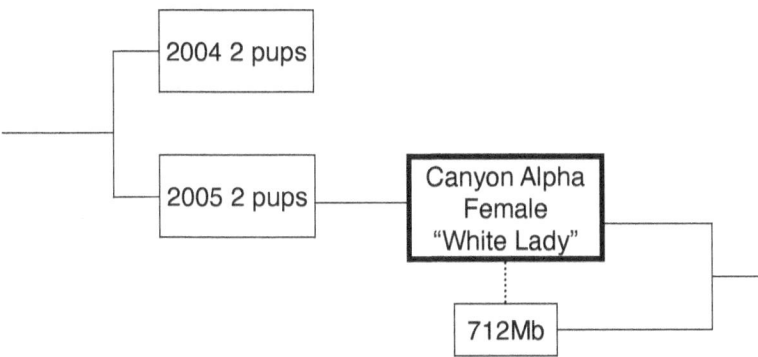

continued on p.18

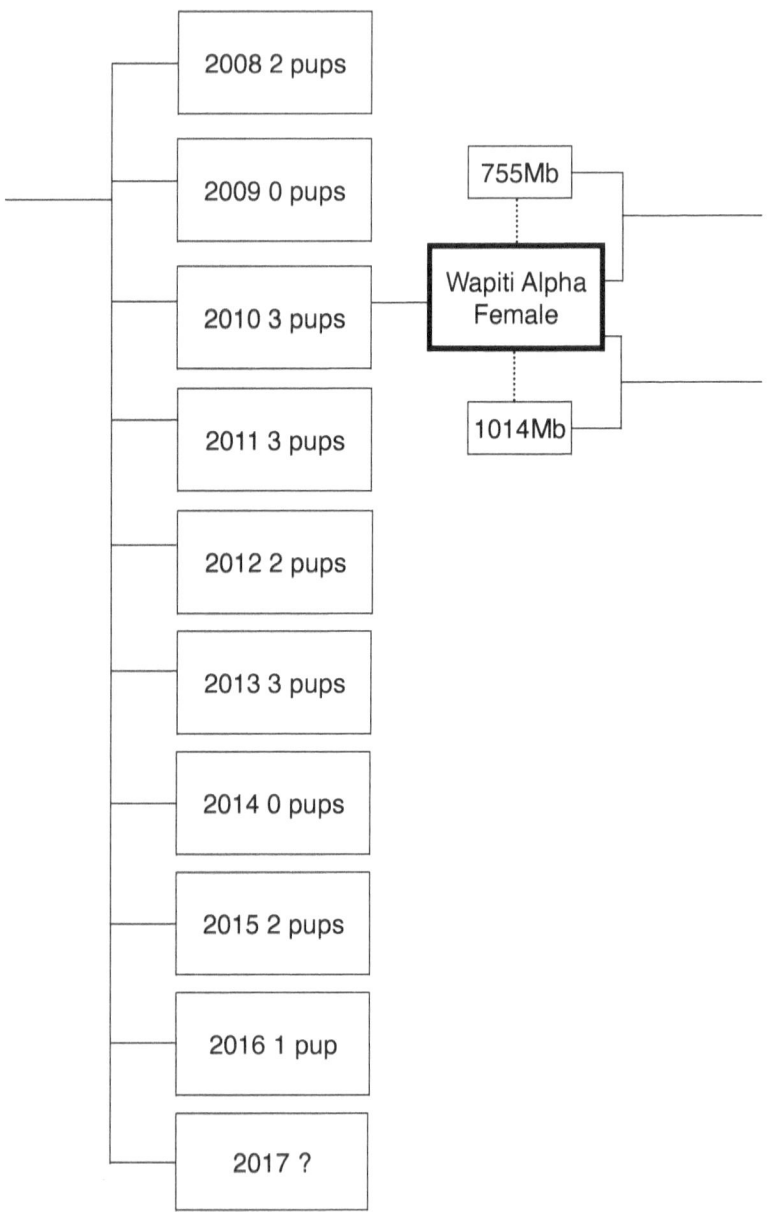

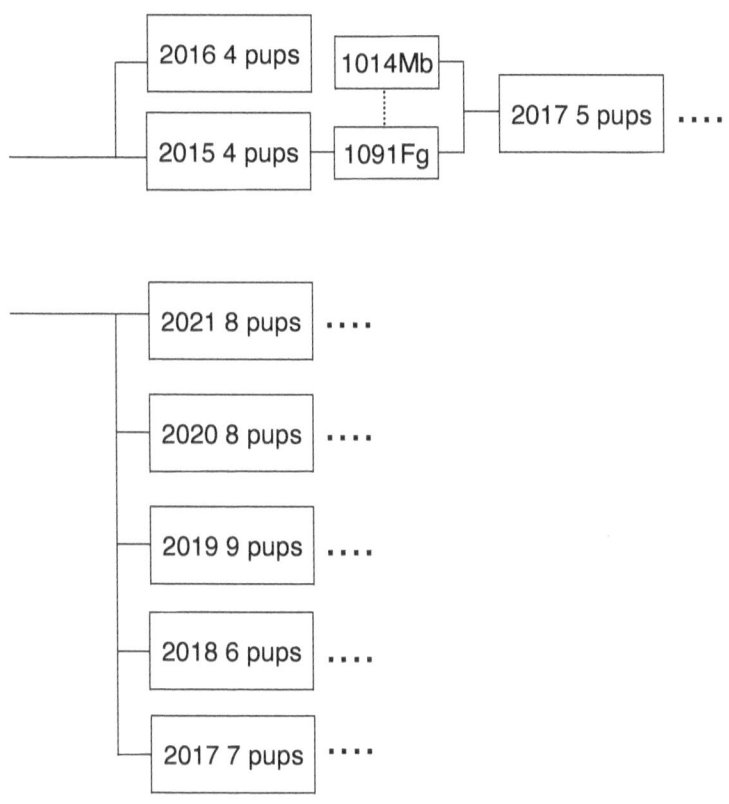

Wolves from this lineage continue in Yellowstone National Park and beyond.

The animal moved slowly but steadily across the snow, barely discernable from its surroundings of white, brown and gray—the colors of late winter in Yellowstone National Park. It stopped, then started again; a tiny spot in the distance surrounded by an eerie fog that made the creature appear to be walking on air.

A frost-bitten wildlife watcher, accustomed to weeks at a time in the park, spotted the movement and eased her truck onto the shoulder of the road. A few more vehicles soon pulled in behind her. Bundled-up people stepped out, careful not to slam doors, five or six at first, whispering to one another. Then more cars crept up and crunched to a halt. Their occupants quietly unloaded spotting scopes and set up cameras on tripods.

"What are you seeing?" A driver with Florida plates almost went past, but rolled down his window at the last minute to see if stopping was worth his time. The man didn't know a wolf jam when he saw one.

"A white wolf. It's pretty rare," someone said. "Hurry."

Florida pulled over.

Low voices mumbled something about the Nez Perce pack that he didn't quite catch. The man tugged his stocking cap down over his ears, removed his glasses and squinted through cheap binoculars. Someone offered him a gander through a high-powered scope.

"Wow." He watched the wolf until it faded into the milky vapor.

"I've heard about these white wolves, I just never thought I'd see one."

Chapter One
The yellow ear tag

The phone rang, breaking the silence. I'd been sitting at my typewriter staring out the window at the flat whiteness. It had snowed seven inches overnight in Montana's East Helena valley, which meant I was stuck doing paperwork. I was a federal trapper who had become the wolf management specialist for Wildlife Services, the U.S. Department of Agriculture agency that handles complaints about wildlife. I spent most of my time on the road examining dead livestock and dealing with wild predators when they were to blame, but today I was home in my aluminum trailer that also functioned as my office.

Joe Fontaine was on the other end of the line. Fontaine worked for the U.S. Fish and Wildlife Service in Helena, and he had news: a pair of wolves had been seen near Augusta. I wasn't surprised. Wolves had been appearing here and there in Montana since 1979, but the outcome was always the same: they showed up, and they were killed. No one seemed to be in the mood to have wolves back on the landscape, not now that the West had been turned over to livestock. It was 1993, and the caretaker of the state's Sun River

Wildlife Management Area/Game Range had called Joe after watching two wolves devour an elk carcass. It was one week after Valentine's Day, peak breeding time for wolves.

"You wanna try and put collars on them?" Joe asked.

This wasn't a question, really. Of course I would.

At this time the feds were doing a careful dance, and I found myself in the middle of it. The U.S. Fish and Wildlife Service had spent the past thirteen years producing stacks of the research and documents necessary to perform a wolf reintroduction in the Northern Rocky Mountains. While in theory they could just let the animals walk here on their own and call it natural recovery, many wildlife scientists believed reintroduction was the only possible way to restore wolf populations in a reasonable amount of time.

In the meantime, however, wolves had already begun to wander here on their own from Canada.

Dealing with problem wolves—and angry ranchers—was something I'd been doing since 1987 when naturally-occurring wolves were crossing the border from Canada into the U.S. more and more frequently. The feds decided that someone needed to work across agency lines to calm the friction of these situations. I turned out to be that person. I never set out to work with wolves, I didn't even apply for the job; the bosses at Wildlife Services assigned this work to me.

Everything having to do with wolves in my life occurred by chance. At one time, I thought I'd stay forever in my home state of Iowa, banding ducks, hunting pheasants and doing taxidermy. Ending up in Montana was a fluke. When I came west, I got off the train in Wolf Point, which may have been a bit of foreshadowing, but I didn't think anything of it. I had taken a temporary job in 1973 trapping skunks in Plentywood. From there I had one gig after another, all having to do with problem varmints. I ended up in Helena in 1975 as a trapper, then a supervisor, for Animal Damage Control, later Wildlife Services. When wolves started showing up, I was in the right place at the right time. Some people might say the wrong time, but I felt like I was cut out for this work.

People with many more university degrees than I suggested the influx of wolves from Canada would result in natural recolonization, and that reintroduction was unnecessary. I disagreed. Wolves may have been successfully crossing the border, but they were picked off as fast as they arrived. Without some help, they would never have gotten a toe-hold and established themselves. If the public wasn't killing them, the feds were, and I was the guy who was routinely sent to kill or capture wild wolves at the same time they were being considered for reintroduction.

I established my opinion very early, based on the many control actions I conducted and everything I saw and heard. I believed the only way to create a successful wolf population in Montana and Idaho in our lifetimes was to reintroduce them in large numbers. The situation was a legal and bureaucratic tangle, and the fights were far from over.

In the meantime, I was the dog catcher on my way to Augusta.

I packed a bag and called Doug Getz, a helicopter pilot for Montana Fish, Wildlife and Parks. I'd known Doug for years. We arrived at the state hangar in Helena and waited for the snow to quit. Getz and I had already played a couple of rounds of cribbage when the call came that skies would be clearing in the next hour or so. When they did, we rolled the Hughes 500 onto the tarmac and took off.

The day went from gray to brilliant as we flew. I thought of all the reports I'd seen in my agency's files: a half dozen lone wolves killed in Montana since 1964, some of them after the federal Endangered Species Act had gone into effect in 1973. This seemed crazy to me. What was this law for if we were just going to keep killing these animals? Perhaps radio collars could help protect them.

I checked and re-checked my dart gun. My mind was a jumble. I wanted to enjoy the flight, but I had too many things to think about. Below us, deer, elk and the occasional coyote scampered away from our noisy machine.

I'd heard for the past four years about a lone wolf in this part of Montana. The wolf wintered deep in "The Bob," as this area was called, short for the federal Bob Marshall Wilderness. The lonesome traveler covered hundreds of square miles of backcountry, living on mule deer and elk or scavenging whatever it could. The feds were calling it the Benchmark wolf after a nearby landmark. Maybe the wolf we were after today was this one, and perhaps it had found a mate.

Soon Getz set us down in a swirl of diamond dust. The snow was dry and powdery, covering the immense game range and beyond—perfect conditions for tracking wolves, even from the air. But it also seemed like a tall order to find two wolves in this vastness. Luckily the whole area was closed to the public in winter or we might have been dodging skiers, snowmobiles and who knew what else. We met the ground crew, prepared a few darts and took a side door off the chopper so I could have a clearer shot. Then we took off into the sparkling air.

I didn't have a lot of experience darting wolves from a helicopter, but on the other hand, no one else did either. Up until this day, I had darted five wolves on five attempts. That was a hundred percent success rate, I figured. If we could find the wolves and get darts in them, we would deliver them to the ground crew, and those folks would do the rest. The VHF radio collars we used for wolves were bulky and ugly, and they weighed about a pound—about one percent of a wolf's body weight.

We had discovered years earlier that these collars worked as a kind of life insurance policy against poaching, and such incidents dropped off considerably once wolves started wearing them. Apparently, some people thought low-flying planes were the feds spying on potential wolf-killers. The collars also gave us masses of information on the whereabouts of a pack or an individual wolf, but only while the batteries held out, which was about three years.

The crew members moved their trucks closer to the game range headquarters and waited. This is where we intended to land and hand off wolves, if we could find them. Getz took us up, and we flew back and forth in transects less than a hundred feet above the snow, which was polka-dotted with thousands of elk tracks. The elk were bunched in great herds, nervously watching our every move.

Trying to pick wolf prints out of this mess was going to be tough. The Rocky Mountain Front loomed before us, rising steeply from the prairie. Between us and those jagged mountains lay miles of patchy, timbered foothills. Wolves in there would be impossible to see. We needed some luck.

We flew to the outer fringes of the elk tracks, and I suddenly saw tracks that didn't match anything else around them. Wolf? They were round and lay in a straight, deliberate line headed toward the horizon.

"Circle back!" I blurted.

We crept along, hovering low and found the prints again. They were enormous, with distinct toenail impressions, which ruled out a mountain lion. Another set of tracks paralleled the ones we were following. Two wolves. I was certain.

"Can you see those two dots out there?" Getz's question crackled in my headset. I looked at him, but he was looking straight ahead.

About a mile distant, two creatures stood still against the white backdrop. Getz accelerated like a Corvette and the chase was on. Freezing wind whipped at me through the open helicopter door, and I repositioned the dart gun that was resting between my knees. I felt for the darts inside my coat pocket, where I'd been keeping them warm. I would wait until we were closer before hanging out the door for a shot.

The closer we got, the bigger the dots got. Two wolves, a large whitish-colored one and a smaller black one stood motionless until they realized we were after them. The black one dashed west toward the forested foothills, its tail flowing straight out behind it.

The nearly-white wolf was enormous, with a neck slightly darker than its body. It hesitated, not knowing which way to run, alternating glances at us and at its fleeing mate. I pushed a dart into the chamber.

"What do you want to do?" Getz asked.

"Go for that light one." This animal likely was the male. His size gave him away. Now his indecision would make him an easy target.

The wolf turned and loped south, perhaps decoying us away from his mate. Getz eased the helicopter up to the wolf as it entered short pines. The deeper drifts of snow here slowed him down. I took aim as we hovered about twenty feet above the animal, and the dart hit him squarely above the left hip, telltale pink yarn at the end of the dart peeking out of the wolf's winter coat.

As we passed over the wolf, a tiny flash of yellow caught my eye.

"Did you see his ear?" Yes, Getz had seen it too.

We banked away and circled in front of the heavy timber to keep the now-drugged wolf from heading there. The wolf stopped, then turned to run the other way. Shortly he was wobbling and taking smaller steps. He paused, his head moving from side to side, and finally fell over.

We stayed away another five minutes, letting the wolf become totally immobilized. Getz used the time to find a place to land where the rotor blades would have good clearance.

The wolf was definitely a male, and as big up close as he had seemed far away. I rolled back his lips to get a look at his teeth. I guessed him to be about five years old. His eyes were wide open, staring blankly. His tongue hung out of his mouth. Getz examined the yellow plastic ear tag. It was chipped and stained, with only part of its original number remaining. We lifted the animal in a heave-ho and put him on the back seat of the helicopter. I covered his eyes and checked his vitals to make sure he was OK. He was the largest wolf I had ever seen.

We made a beeline toward the ground crew, and as we approached I could see them trying to gauge our success. They didn't look optimistic. I let them think the worst until the last minute, when I gave Fontaine a thumbs-up. It took a few of us to get the wolf onto a tarp, then onto the hook of a portable scale. He weighed one hundred twenty-two pounds. The crew fitted him with a collar. As for the ear tag, no one had a clue.

This big male wolf would be released here. On a clear day without mountains in the way, his collar would transmit for twenty to thirty miles. The crew packed up and left, but Fontaine stayed behind, keeping an eye on the drugged wolf. Once the animal got his wits back and was on his feet, he was gone, slipping away into the cold, blue evening to find his mate.

One collar was enough to keep track of both of them, because we knew they were traveling together. These two would now be called the Sawtooth pack, or more specifically, "the Sawtooth male" and "the Sawtooth female."

I crossed my fingers and hoped they would stay out of trouble.

Chapter 2
Early Returns

The mystery of the yellow ear tag was soon solved.

In 1988, Mike Jimenez, a graduate student at the University of Montana, had studied a group of eight wolves just over the Canadian border north of Glacier Park. They were known as the Wigwam pack, and he accidently trapped two pups—a male and a female—too small to radio-collar. Jimenez attached yellow ear tags with identification numbers to each pup and turned them loose.

The Wigwams disappeared before Jimenez could finish his research. He presented his thesis anyway, but never could discover what happened to the pack. A year later, two U.S. Forest Service biologists, Pat Finnegan and Seth Diamond, searched for wolves as part of an official survey and discovered a single set of wolf tracks. They named the unseen animal the Benchmark wolf after a nearby land feature.

This wolf turned out to be a survivor of the Wigwam pack, resurfacing along the eastern edge of "The Bob," short for the Bob

Marshall Wilderness, more than one hundred fifty miles from his family's original territory. The wolf's identity was confirmed by an enduring yellow ear tag. Now, in 1993, he had been caught again, and given yet another name: the Sawtooth male.

Long before the Benchmark wolf appeared, a handful of scientists had been searching for wolves in the Northern Rockies. They often found signs of the animals even though wolves were considered mostly extinct in the lower 48 states by the 1930s. Bob Ream of the University of Montana began the ambitious Wolf Ecology Project in 1973 to search for and document wild wolves that had withstood Americans' attempts to get rid of them. The project began the same year wolves were given legal protection under the federal Endangered Species Act. The American people had seen the light. After fifty years, the government that killed off wolves did an about-face.

Ream's students and colleagues were the first to capture and radio collar wolves in Montana and southern Canada. Diane Boyd, one of Ream's students, followed wolf tracks along Montana's North Fork Flathead River in 1985, leading her to radio-collar descendants of the previously known Magic pack just outside the west boundary of Glacier National Park. These were the first wolves to den in Montana after an absence of more than five decades.

Canada allowed trapping and hunting of wolves, but its wildlife officials acknowledged they didn't have much control over illegal poisonings, something that happened with sobering regularity. Even the Canadian government was engaged in the poisoning of wolves, much like the U.S. government had been.

Scientists knew the Magic, Wigwam and other packs were making forays into Montana, but they certainly weren't breeding there; pups were being born in British Columbia and Alberta. It didn't take long for this to change. In just a few years the Browning pack set up a home territory in northern Montana, then the Marion pack, then others.

Ream's researchers worried about their collared wolves until the animals returned to the Montana portions of their territories. Here the wolves found an idyllic setting: few livestock, and the wolves had federal protection. But this habitat was nothing like the rest of Montana, where livestock was everywhere. I agreed with the federal scientists: wolves would never be able to re-establish themselves in any kind of meaningful way unless we helped them.

Far away from Montana's verdant borderland, the federal government was churning out documents and holding inner-circle meetings about how to bring back wolves and get this iconic species off the federal endangered species list. The endless piles of paperwork included a one hundred nineteen-page wolf recovery plan published in 1987, written by an assortment of scientists. An accompanying document was published in 1988, *Wolf Control Guidelines, Northern Rocky Mountains*.

The latter document quickly went from draft to final. There was not a lot of hand-wringing over the fact that wolves that killed livestock would not be tolerated. The control plan was what got most ranchers onboard with the idea of reintroduction. They wanted a promise in writing that we would do something about problem wolves. Natural recolonization didn't necessarily come with that kind of assurance.

This was a sticking point for some conservation groups, and they scoffed at the "kill-them-to-save-them" federal attitude. Let them come back on their own, they said. But wolves had never made a comeback in the many decades since they were obliterated simply because people continued to shoot and poison them as fast as the animals arrived. Adopting a belief that wolves would eventually recolonize by themselves in the Northern Rockies was, in my opinion, a way to let extinction stand. We needed to do something big—really big—to give them a fighting chance.

Still, this reintroduction concept was a brash idea. Nothing like it had ever been attempted. The wheels of government continued grinding and soon a plan was in place. The U.S. Fish and Wildlife Service would bring wolves from Canada to Yellowstone National Park and central Idaho once a year for five years.

In the end, we got the job done in two.

In 1995 and 1996, the park received a total of 31 wolves. Idaho received 35. A glorious experiment in wolf recovery was underway.

But in my world, wolves had already been making things complicated for quite a while.

Chapter 3
Searching for Solutions

After the capture of the Sawtooth male, I went back to my usual routine of examining dead cows and sheep and determining how they had died.

It was early 1994, and wolves had been making appearances in Montana for more than twelve years. Montana is a big place, and as a federal trapper and supervisor of trappers, it seemed I drove every one of its roads—dirt, gravel and paved.

I knew my agency was the hired gun of the livestock industry, and I wasn't too far off in assuming that Wildlife Services—formerly and more accurately known as Animal Damage Control—opposed wolf recovery of any sort. Wildlife Services managers were worried the presence of wolves, even the rumor of their presence, would screw up their coyote-killing campaigns. They would have to pull up their traps, deactivate their M-44 sodium cyanide devices, and watch their step to be in compliance with federal regulations that protected wolves.

Keeping predators at bay for the benefit of ranchers was central to this agency's existence, and its employees were quite aware of this fact. Wildlife Services personnel in my neck of the woods believed they worked not for the public, but for private enterprise: ranchers. Reintroduce wolves? Are people insane? That was Wildlife Services' group-think. For this reason, my bosses wanted me to keep tabs on this emerging wolf issue and changed my job title to "wolf specialist." I'd already been doing the job, minus the title, for a few years. At some point I became so immersed in the work that my life and my job became one and the same.

I found myself a combination of dog catcher and coroner. The mere mention of wolves was creating an uproar, and I was regularly summoned to look at dead animals, often while a rancher stood over my shoulder telling me what to think. My phone used to ring with calls about coyotes eating sheep, or a bear getting into someone's beehives, or skunks breeding under a barn. Now the calls were all about wolves.

In 1994, four dozen naturally-occurring wolves, including five breeding pairs, existed in Northwest Montana, and everything dead was blamed on them. Newspaper reporters wrote about the reappearance of wolves, and as with anything new and uncertain, public hysteria kicked in. Cow carcasses lying forgotten in a far-flung pasture took on ominous meanings. Bands of sheep threw themselves into deep coulees at the sight of a wolf. Domestic livestock died every day before wolves showed up, but now there was something new to blame, and many citizens blamed wolves.

My job had gone from ordinary to outlandish, and my phone rang day and night, even more on weekends and holidays.

Many of the animal carcasses I was asked to examine were in advanced stages of decomposition. I'd had a bit of forensics training from experts at the University of Montana, but I mostly had to figure this out for myself. I learned quickly that I needed fresh bodies to examine, or I would not be able to determine a cause of death.

My first priority was to find ways to get whoever discovered a carcass to call me sooner than later, and to get people to cover the carcass or protect it in some way to prevent further scavenging. I didn't like the idea that a single species was being blamed for everything dead. Sure, some dead livestock were victims of wolves, but I wanted to find ways to solve problems without always having to kill predators. We humans are supposed to be smarter than animals, so we needed to act like it.

The truth is that cattle and sheep succumb less to predators than to disease, birthing problems, old age, infirmities, poison and accidents. When a predator was to blame, my prime suspects were coyotes, bears, mountain lions, domestic dogs and golden eagles, mostly because there are many more of them than wolves. In fact, wolves didn't usually make my list.

I thought my reasoning made sense, but I was being pressured by ranchers and my agency to blame wolves for killing livestock, even when there was no proof. Each predator, however, leaves a kill-signature. This was something I'd discovered by looking at a lot of carcasses, and most of them were not wolf signatures. The more dead and injured livestock I examined, the more comfortable I became as a forensics man—the only one around. There were already wolves on the Montana landscape, and the 1995 reintroduction was coming fast. Once wolves were on the ground in Yellowstone and Idaho, I was certain the wolf issue would heat up even more.

Once wolves start killing livestock, they seldom stop no matter how much they're harassed. We thought we were giving wolves a chance to start over by moving them, but it was disastrous in almost every case: dead wolves, dead cattle and sheep, lots of money spent, hard feelings, bad press. We had to do better. We needed training and equipment. No agency had the knowledge or budget to deal with wolf issues, no matter how many plans and reports had been created. This was part of the reason that, in the summer of 1988, the U.S. Fish and Wildlife Service hired Ed Bangs as the Northern Rockies Wolf Recovery Coordinator. He was to oversee all things having to do with wolves outside of national parks.

When the Department of the Interior advertised the job, no one applied except Bangs. He was a biologist in Alaska who once had taken the scenic road home through Helena, Montana and was dumbfounded by the beauty of the country. When the wolf job opened, he jumped at it, not because he was interested in wolves particularly, but because he wanted to live in Helena. How hard could a Montana winter be after living in Alaska?

I met Bangs in July 1988 and gave him a summary of the latest wolf dramas. I'd been running all over the state for a couple of years chasing down reports. I was relieved at his arrival. Bangs was now my buffer, and when I had to "control" wolves, I sent critics to him.

Bangs asked about equipment and immobilizing drugs. We had none. He immediately ordered what he thought we needed, including a copy of the 1988 wolf control guidelines.

I began modifying my own traps because I had none that could catch and hold a wolf without injuring it. Coyote traps were too small. Bear traps were too big. I started making phone calls, and Roy McBride in Texas, a remnant trapper from another era, became my supplier. He sent me No. 7s, which had jaws about seven inches in diameter when open, large enough to accommodate a wolf's foot. I filed the trap teeth down to nubs in my machine shed, hoping to keep the steel from puncturing skin. A wolf lives by its feet, and I didn't want to be the guy who screwed them up.

Once Bangs was on the scene he instructed Wildlife Services to handle wolves with care. He OK'd the occasional harassment and killing of wolves that were causing problems, but Bangs knew such actions put the U.S. Fish and Wildlife Service on thin ice legally: wolves that had been trickling in from Canada were fully protected under the Endangered Species Act once they touched American soil. Lucky for Bangs, no one sued.

Based on the belief that wolf management was about to get very busy, Bangs was directed to hire an assistant. He picked Joe Fontaine, a guy who could talk with anyone.

"We had no idea what we were doing," Bangs said later. "The wolves dictated everything. We just reacted."

Along with Fontaine's hire, the feds added Steve Fritts as chief scientist for the Northern Rocky Mountain wolf recovery program.

"The pressure was to sit at your desk," Bangs said. But he had no intention of doing that. He'd been hired to run the wolf program, and he made short work of turning it into a field operation. He had me on speed-dial.

I was reassured by Bangs' confidence as he made decisions that got wolf recovery off the ground, but I wasn't sure how to put a smiley face on the fact that I might have to kill more wolves before reintroduction ever got started. Something had to improve. I dreaded the next phone call. So far, everything we had done with these animals had been a disaster. Wolves killed livestock, and we killed the wolves. If we didn't kill them, we moved them, which disoriented them and caused packs to break up and pups to die. In my estimation, this was failure.

By the time the Sawtooth wolves appeared in 1993, I had decided we had to achieve a better outcome.

We just had to.

Chapter 4
The Wild Sawtooth Wolves

The Sawtooth pack may have been given an official name, but most of the time Forest Service biologists Seth Diamond and Pat Finnegan unofficially called the pair "Bonnie and Clyde" because these two wolves caused mayhem wherever they went.

The naming of wolf packs was something that evolved on its own. Biologists decided early on to choose a particular landmark —in this case Sawtooth Ridge—to identify individual packs. And while some packs were named after geographic land features, others were named after the watersheds they frequented, or a nearby town. Lone wolves that showed up on their own and were captured were never given names, only collar frequencies or ear tag numbers. Mostly we called these wild individuals by their pack names—the Marion female, the Browning male.

In March 1993, Diamond and Finnegan, who had followed early tracks in the Bob Marshall Wilderness, set up meetings with ranchers who were unknowingly hosting Bonnie and Clyde. I knew some of these ranchers from years of grizzly bear issues, but

I was always eager to meet new folks. Joe Fontaine and I often made these kinds of visits together, and this time all of us met at the Augusta Ranger Station. This group was a mix of ranchers and neighbors of large parcels of land that had been in the same families for generations. Nearly all of them ran cattle on thousands of acres of private and public lands along the Rocky Mountain Front. No area is more beautiful, partly because the land hosted so much wildlife. No wonder the Sawtooth wolves wanted to live here.

The men were friendly, and even though they wished the wolves would pick a different home territory, they weren't hostile about the animals' presence, and they didn't want them killed. We exchanged phone numbers and promised to share radio-tracking information. In exchange, they wanted discretion and to be kept informed. We shook on it, and all of them gave us permission to come and go as we needed.

Several weeks later, four Sawtooth pups were born on the LF Ranch, one of the stunning properties we'd predicted the wolves might pick. Bonnie stayed close, keeping to a four square-mile area around the den. The land was brimming with white-tailed deer. We tracked the collared Sawtooth male, Clyde, far and wide. I wasn't sure whether he was hunting or just bumming around.

In May, Fontaine and I were called to the LF to examine two calf carcasses. Larry Davis, a state game warden, was there as well. I didn't think the calves were fresh kills, and for that reason I couldn't link them to Bonnie and Clyde, but the wolves were certainly scavenging the leftovers.

I met with foreman Tim Tew and we talked about the flourishing pack. He wasn't too concerned about the LF, but he worried about his neighbors. Their operations were smaller and probably couldn't afford the losses that wolves might inflict.

Tew was a cowboy, but an unusual one. He liked wildlife and took a strong interest in the wolves and resident grizzlies that frequented the ranch. I valued his insight. Tew thought having wolves around was pretty neat. "Keep talking to people," he said. "It'll buy you a lot."

July came and went. The LF's hired hands had become well-versed in the comings and goings of the ranch's wolves. The cowboys moved cattle to avoid disturbing the fledgling pack—and to avoid feeding the wolves fresh hamburger. Neighboring ranchers said they didn't want to know the den's location, and I guess they never noticed it was right next to the LF's main road. Maybe these folks wanted plausible deniability.

Soon it didn't matter. Bonnie and Clyde moved their pups to a rendezvous site a couple of miles away on the adjacent state-owned Sun River Game Range. By autumn, biologists had radio-collared two of the pups. The juvenile animals weighed about fifty pounds each. When the first snow flew, outfitters and hunters caught occasional glimpses of the Sawtooth wolves and eagerly reported their sightings at check-stations.

But this kind of calm never lasts.

On February 22, 1994, my phone rang. It was Pat Finnegan. Bonnie and Clyde had killed a two-day old calf at the LF.

Tracks in the snow told the story. A short distance from the ranch house, a single wolf bit a small calf in the left flank, leaving deep wounds. The mother cow attacked the wolf, but in her panic trampled her baby, breaking at least three of its ribs and stepping on the calf's abdomen. When the ranch foreman approached the scene, a black wolf ran away.

The ranch and its neighbors insisted this attack be kept low-key. No publicity, they said. The conservation group Defenders of Wildlife sent a check, and that was the extent of the encounter.

We could do nothing to keep the Sawtooth wolves away from cattle, if that's where they wanted to be. This had always been the problem in the past—at Browning, Marion and in the Ninemile. We had few harassment techniques at the time. We were all ears if someone had new and better ideas, but no one did. New ideas were still a long way off.

Shortly before the wolves killed the LF calf, Defenders of Wildlife announced publicly it had paid "an Augusta, Montana cattle rancher" five thousand dollars for allowing wolves to raise pups on the private ranchland. All the locals seemed to know about the wolves, even though it was supposed to be a secret. The payment was much more than a few calves were worth. Maybe Defenders hoped the money would encourage tolerance.

In April 1994, about a month after the LF depredation, the Sawtooth wolves killed a calf on the neighboring Weisner ranch. The wolves kept harassing the herds, causing young calves to break legs in the wolf-induced stampedes, and mothers to trample their newborns trying to fend off the predators. JT Weisner was losing patience with the Sawtooths.

So was Ed Bangs.

He wanted two yearling wolves—any two—relocated. Bangs was trying to preserve this pack if he could, but he was ready to have me kill them if necessary. Maybe removing two young wolves would do the trick.

I called pilots Ron Gipe and Dave Hoerner. These guys were experienced at animal capture, though Gipe and I had to learn the ropes together when it came to chasing wolves in a helicopter. It was something we would do many times in the years to come.

The LF's private airstrip became the headquarters of our operation. The ground crew unloaded metal kennels and got everything ready. I prepared tranquilizer darts while Hoerner circled above us in his fixed-wing plane, looking for wolves. In a few minutes he detected Clyde's collar.

Gipe and I were soon in the air, and quickly found the wolves in a forested thicket a mile away, halfway between the LF and the Weisner ranches. The wolves took off when they heard us coming, and one ran right past the ground crew.

The dense brush made capture tough. I couldn't shoot unless a wolf ran through an open meadow. Gipe was patient and persistent and I eventually darted a seventy-eight-pound female and a ninety-eight-pound male.

The crew collected blood samples, measured and weighed the wolves, then fastened ear tags to each animal and fitted them with radio collars. Soon the wolves were on their way to Glacier National Park. Montana officials were nervous about letting this pair go anywhere on state land, and complained about it often and loudly to the feds. It's why these wolves ended up in Glacier. Years earlier the Marion and Ninemile wolves had been taken there, too.

Fontaine shared the radio frequencies with Mike Madel, the state's grizzly bear manager, hoping that a Sawtooth wolf or two might show up during one of Madel's bear monitoring flights. A short time later, Madel found Clyde resting near a herd of angus cattle on the LF ranch. The low flying plane caused Clyde to stand up and stretch, drawing the attention of the herd. In a final glimpse, Madel saw the wolf running into tall timber, tail tucked, with the cattle in hot pursuit.

After the upheaval of capture, the Sawtooth wolves stopped harassing livestock.

In June, Clyde's collar fell off. Pat Finnegan searched for it in the rugged hills and eventually found it near Sawtooth Ridge. Apparently, Clyde's packmates had chewed it off fairly close to where we originally caught the old boy. Without a collar we had no clue to his whereabouts. Clyde was never seen again. According to local scuttlebutt, one of the locals shot him as he lay on a grassy knoll near a road, but his body was never found.

In the same month that Clyde disappeared, Finnegan saw six wolf pups near the old den site—one black and five gray. Another biologist also had recently collared a yearling female that accompanied Bonnie. More ways to keep track of the Sawtooths.

Local ranchers were growing tense. They questioned whether sending two wolves to Glacier would make any difference, but we wanted to deal with problem wolves in small bites. Maybe if we incrementally reduced the pack's size, they would be under less pressure to find food, and there would be fewer livestock deaths. We were all on a steep learning curve.

In the meantime, we'd lost a place to send wayward wolves. The negative publicity surrounding earlier relocations gave Glacier National Park officials cold feet. They waved off any more transplants. They'd said yes to the release of livestock-killing wolves three times in the past five years, but political heat was melting their resolve. Send wolves somewhere else, they said.

Ranchers who grazed cattle near the boundaries of Glacier breathed a collective sigh of relief when the two relocated Sawtooth wolves left the park and trotted north into Canada. There they had no protection, so no one was surprised to hear they were both killed. The female died at the hands of an Alberta man who feared for his colts. The male wolf survived for a while, traveling the Belly River drainage through Waterton Lakes National Park. He went north for another two hundred miles before his life ended on a trapline.

The whole incident was chalked up as disappointment and futility. Defenders of Wildlife sent checks totaling more than seventeen hundred dollars for the Montana calves killed by the Sawtooth wolves. But because nothing with wolves is ever simple, that wasn't the end of the story.

Not long after the Sawtooths started their killing spree in Augusta, the final paperwork of federal wolf reintroduction was signed and published. The final Environmental Impact Statement weighed a couple of pounds.

Soon Yellowstone National Park and Central Idaho would have wolves.

In October 1994, capture and veterinary teams for this historic event were selected. Bangs wanted me on the capture side of things.

My four-week assignment in Alberta began in mid-November with a two-day drive from Helena through a blizzard. My job was to coordinate with local fur trappers who were used to killing wolves for their thick winter pelts. Instead, they were paid to keep the wolves alive. The animals were collared and released so they and their families could later be found, captured and delivered to their new homes.

The actual moving of the wolves from Alberta and British Columbia to the U.S. happened in January of both years, 1995 and 1996. The operation was a logistical puzzle, and several glitches—non-existent contracts with trappers, distrust of feds and inertia on our part—nearly killed the whole exercise, but it worked, if only by the seat of our pants.

The fourteen wolves shipped from Alberta to Yellowstone in 1995, were family groups of various sizes. All were kept in enclosures of heavy wire fence for ten weeks to shed them of their tendency to wander back to Canada.

The packs were named for the locales of their pens and kept out of sight of humans to keep them wild. Crystal Creek, Rose Creek and Soda Butte were the names of the park's first wolf packs. In 1996, an additional seventeen wolves were flown from British Columbia to the park. They would be known as the Chief Joseph, Druid Peak, Lone Star, and Nez Perce packs.

The reintroduction of wolves held great significance to the Nez Perce Tribe, whose elders waited on the airport tarmac in Missoula to bless the return of the wolves as the animals made their journey toward Central Idaho. In Yellowstone, the pen that held the Nez Perce pack straddled Nez Perce Creek in a remote area near Old Faithful.

Yellowstone's wolves had been captured just before their normal breeding season and they lost no time breeding in their holding pens. Because of this we thought more introductions might not be necessary. In the end, the 1996 capture was the final one. Besides, park biologists already had their hands full with thirty-one wolves.

It was just the beginning.

The early-spring release of the Nez Perce pack in 1996 was the beginning of a saga that no one fully anticipated—and it involved the free-wheeling Sawtooth wolves two hundred miles away.

Chapter 5
The Plan

A year after sending two yearling Sawtooth wolves to Glacier National Park, I was able to capture two more from this pack. They were the only two we could find, a one hundred-pound gray and an eighty-five-pound black. Both were yearling males, and both would wear radio collars from now on as we tried to figure out what was going on with the Sawtooths.

The black one had a stiff and withered rear leg with a weeping abscess, apparently from an old gunshot wound. The ground crew discovered this wolf also had a case of mange, which I hadn't noticed as I heaved it into the helicopter. This stressed and underweight wolf became known casually as Limp Leg. The crew gave him an injection of antibiotics and an anti-parasite medicine, both of which were routinely used on captured wolves. When the two recovered from sedation, they wandered back to their packmates.

The radio collar information on these two indicated they were not visiting the den site, and no one saw pups. This meant the pack didn't breed in 1995. Stockmen in the area reported only one dead calf that entire summer, and it was not a verified wolf kill. For the time being, the Sawtooth pack was not desperate to feed youngsters.

But almost exactly a year later, in March 1996, wolves killed two small calves on the LF Ranch. Tim Tew and game warden Davis watched me peel the skin off the carcasses. The evidence of wolf predation was overwhelming: crushing bite wounds in the calves' flanks, torn flesh, hemorrhage, and wolf tracks in the snow. Even as wolves were being released in Yellowstone more than two hundred miles away, this was most certainly the work of the Sawtooths.

Despite this development, and the fact that the Sawtooth wolves had returned to their old den along the ranch road, the LF was adamant about keeping its wolf troubles out of the newspapers. Defenders of Wildlife quietly paid the ranch nine hundred dollars for the calves. This informal agreement, however, didn't make my supervisor in Billings happy. On the phone he barked in my ear, "If the LF is going to harbor wolves that kill cattle, I'm pulling you out of there."

He made it sound like a fugitive operation for the FBI.

Soon lips were flapping. Members of the Montana Stockgrowers Association now knew all about the Sawtooth wolves, and everyone who had so successfully kept this pack on the down-low was pissed off—especially the Pierce family, who owned the LF ranch.

Ed Bangs couldn't believe what had happened. The presence of wolves at the LF was just too tempting for the anti-wolf Wildlife Services managers. They thought of themselves as the guardians of stockmen. But I thought of myself as a problem-solver, and I wanted to find a way to keep cattle *and* wolves alive. It almost cost me my job.

Montana had a lot of vocal wolf opponents, but also many people who liked wolves and wanted them back on the landscape. One of those people was Bob Ream of the University of Montana.

Ream often used his private airplane to track collared wolves. In mid-August, he flew over the Sawtooth pack's territory with a guest, British author Nicholas Evans. The young writer was in love with the American West. After his meteoric hit, *The Horse Whisperer*, he was at work on another book, this time about wolves returning to the Northern Rocky Mountains. The Sawtooth wolves and the daily drama at the LF Ranch inspired him, and he used this setting as the backdrop of his 1998 novel, *The Loop*. I must have made an impression on Evans, because I ended up as a character in the story: trapper Bill Rimmer. The Sawtooth situation yielded a lot of material for Evans.

Others wanted to get a closer look at the Sawtooth wolves as well. Liz Bradley was a student at the University of Montana working as a summer volunteer for the U.S. Fish and Wildlife Service in Helena. Ed Bangs sent her and another volunteer, Nikki Krisfalusi, to spy on the Sawtooth pack.

Volunteers were the best available source of labor, according to Bangs. They existed on scraps and would live in a cardboard box if they had to. But the Pierce family immediately took to these two women and put them up in a cabin on ranch property. Their budding friendship came with familiar conditions: maintain the family's privacy and respect the wildlife on their property. The conditions also included a request that the women not howl at the Sawtooth wolves in order to locate them; the Pierces thought human howling disrupted the wolves. A similar rule existed in Yellowstone. The Pierces were fans of wildlife and were not interested in taking revenge on animals that offended them. Of course, once the cattle-killing started, all bets were off.

Bradley kept a journal during her stay, and her entries were gold:

> *July 15, 1996—Nikki and I watched the pups for three hours. They're getting big enough so it's hard to differentiate them from the two-year-olds. The most wolves I counted at one time was 13 and from a distance they looked like pups but I'm*

> sure a few of them must've been two-year-olds. But we figured at least 10 of them must have been pups—a very large litter!
>
> *July 16, 1996*—*The Sawtooth pack's den site was located in a patch of trees (located on a vast grassy meadow on an open ridgeline). There were trails throughout the trees and remnants of kills they'd made laying around such as deer jaws and hooves. There were 3 holes that had been dug. The largest hole was 22 inches wide and 17 inches high at the opening. The entrance went in about 4-5 feet and then diverged to both the right and left. This was probably their main entrance....*
>
> *The Sawtooth pack (is) unique from any other pack in Montana in that they're prairie wolves rather than timber wolves. It seems like there's a lot of opportunity for interesting research that could be conducted on this pack since they're the first wolves to recognize the prairie since they were wiped out years ago....*

On August 15, bear manager Mike Madel, on a routine monitoring flight, happened upon a rare sight: three adult wolves attacking a several hundred-pound Hereford calf just over the hill from the LF. Another wolf, accompanied by nine pups, watched from a nearby knoll.

The pilot banked the plane so Madel could get a better look. Several low passes did nothing to drive the wolves away. They ignored the airplane and pulled the calf to the ground. Madel aborted his bear search and reported the incident to me and the local game warden.

The calf belonged to Ray Krone, whose ranch was about two miles from the Sawtooths' den. By the time Madel and warden Davis reached the scene, more than half of the calf had been consumed or carried away.

I arrived in the late afternoon. In addition to the calf remains, we examined three cow carcasses in various stages of decomposition. Madel had noticed these old carcasses during his flights. The animals had not been killed by wolves, but several species of predators, including wolves, were scavenging them.

If Madel hadn't seen the attack on the calf with his own eyes, the Sawtooth pack might have gotten away with it. Three days later, the only evidence left was bone fragments, flattened grass and blood stains.

Krone was not happy.

"I'd shoot one," Krone said of the wolves on his property. "I'd shoot one in a minute." The only reason he didn't was because it might have landed him in jail.

That summer Liz Bradley confirmed what I believed as well: the Sawtooth pack probably had two breeding females because an awful lot of puppies were frolicking in the meadow. I thought there might be a dozen youngsters, and Bradley counted thirteen. That was a lot of mouths to feed, and the easiest way to do that, apparently, was to prey on the slow and clueless cattle.

It was an age-old problem. But now a parallel issue existed on the Krone ranch: dead cattle had been left lying around. Regardless of how they got that way, the carcasses attracted every predator and scavenger for miles.

Many ranchers didn't see a connection between rotting carcasses and big predators—or maybe they didn't care to see. It's still the same today. Cowboys and herders periodically checked on their animals, but no one spent much time thinking about what might be attracting bears and coyotes—and now wolves. My outfit, Wildlife Services, had always taken care of problem predators, so ranchers didn't have to worry about them. Our help was essentially free, which added to their bottom line.

Biologist Madel had recently been promoting a program to move livestock carcasses to higher, more remote areas to keep grizzly bears out of cattle herds. But now wolves were part of the predator mix, and when it came to wolves killing livestock, the solution was generally always the same: kill or move the wolves.

We were heavy-handed with early wolves outside of the Yellowstone and Central Idaho recovery areas. Moving and killing wolves was legally tricky, but Bangs gave me orders, and I carried them out. It seemed odd that north of Interstate 90 and the Missouri River, wolves actually had more legal protections than they did inside of official recovery areas.

Nevertheless, something needed to be done about this Sawtooth bunch; we couldn't let them keep killing cattle. This promise had been the cornerstone of allowing wolves back on the landscape. Besides, we were good at finding a way around the rules.

Every week, newspapers ran front-page stories about wolf reintroduction, and every move we made was under a microscope. The Sawtooth situation was similar to other wolf problems that had been happening for years. If we dilly-dallied, we would lose the confidence of ranchers, and the entire reintroduction experiment might go down in flames.

Our answer to problem wolves outside of reintroduction areas was the 1988 control plan. This was the only legal instrument available to deal with wolves that were fully protected. Inside the reintroduction areas, we used the Endangered Species Act itself, specifically Section 10, "Exceptions."

All of this catching and moving and sometimes killing of wolves was the only way we could save wolves as a whole, which sounds ridiculous, but it was true.

"(Conservationists) wanted reintroduction more than they were opposed to control," Bangs said later. "But if they'd sued us, we probably would have lost."

The wolf control plan was pretty simple: two strikes and you're out. A second attack on livestock meant that adult wolves and their pups could be moved or killed. The only slack in the plan—the only way for us to try and preserve every wolf possible—was to apply control measures incrementally. We hoped this approach would halt depredations and simultaneously let the wolves stay put. It was all case-by-case, however, depending on the size of the pack. Bangs made decisions and didn't worry too much about asking permission. He preferred to beg forgiveness. It was a chaotic time, and sometimes our measures were also chaotic.

When we moved or killed adult wolves, we hoped the pups would survive on their own, although that didn't usually happen. Wolves need the structure of the pack to make it in life. The reintroduction scientists may have known this, but the rest of us didn't. We just did what we had to do, making it up as we went along because we had almost nothing to guide us. The wolves we'd moved in the past—Marion and Ninemile—didn't stay where we put them, and if they didn't starve, get hit by a car or get killed by other wolves, they often got in trouble for killing livestock again. Next to humans, they were—and still are—their own worst enemies.

We learned these lessons the hard way, and soon we would face another test with the Sawtooths.

Just as we were all wringing our hands over the prospect of killing the rest of the pack, Bangs thought up a solution. Yellowstone's new wolves needed more genetic diversity, and a way to add some would be to send the Sawtooth pups there. He struck a bargain with park managers. The Sawtooth adults seemed incorrigible, but the youngsters had not committed any sins against livestock. They were pups, so they were innocents.

Bangs reasoned that Yellowstone workers were still keeping and feeding a few of the reintroduced wolves in some of the acclimation pens. These wolves had similarly been harassing livestock or leaving the park after being released, and were now back in pens to break those behaviors. Adding a few puppies shouldn't make much more work, Bangs said.

We had a plan. Now all we had to do was put it into action.

The Sawtooth male, "Clyde," when he was still known as the Wigwam pup. The yellow ear tag mystery started with this wolf.
(Photo courtesy Mike Jimenez)

Clyde, after I caught him in 1996.
A co-worker in Iowa gave me the nickname "Clyde" when I worked as a biologist for the Iowa Conservation Commission in the 1970s.
(Photo: Carter Niemeyer collection)

A Sawtooth pup in 1996. When the pups were first captured, they each weighed approximately fifty pounds. Wolves are considered "pups" until they are a year old, at which point they become "yearlings."
(Photo courtesy Liz Bradley)

*A Sawtooth adult awaits re-collaring and release.
We used the same metal crates that were used in Canada during
reintroduction, which were equipped with sliding metal panels over the bars.
During the Sawtooth capture the weather was hot so we didn't use the panels.
This wolf took advantage of previously damaged bars, working its head
through the gap.
(Photo courtesy Liz Bradley)*

*A ground crew member gives water to an adult Sawtooth wolf in its crate.
(Photo courtesy Liz Bradley)*

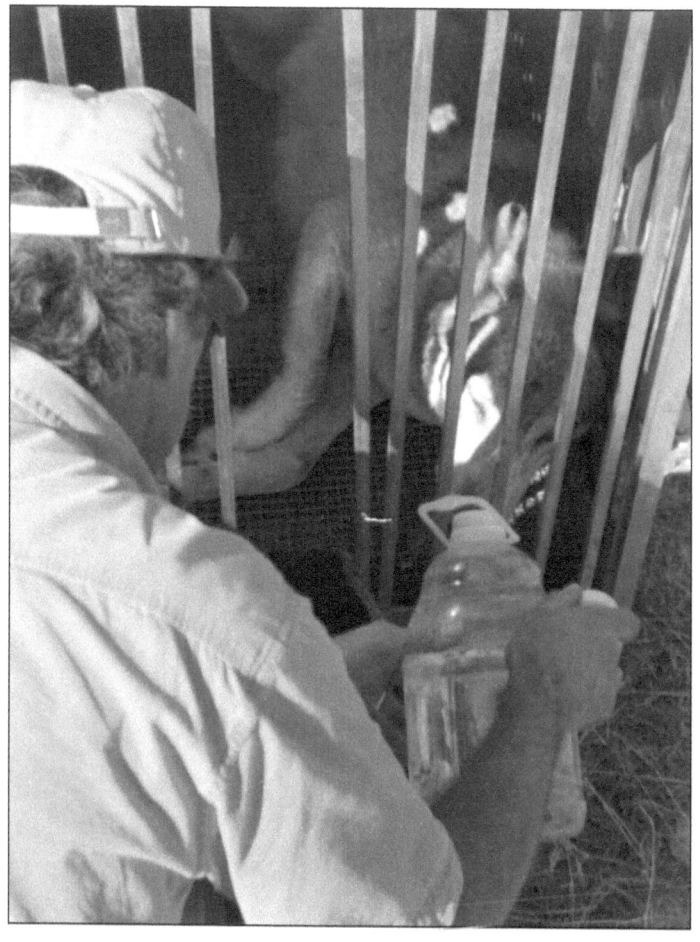

Montana Department of Fish Wildlife and Parks biologist Mike Madel examines a Sawtooth pup after its capture near Augusta, Montana. (Photo courtesy Liz Bradley)

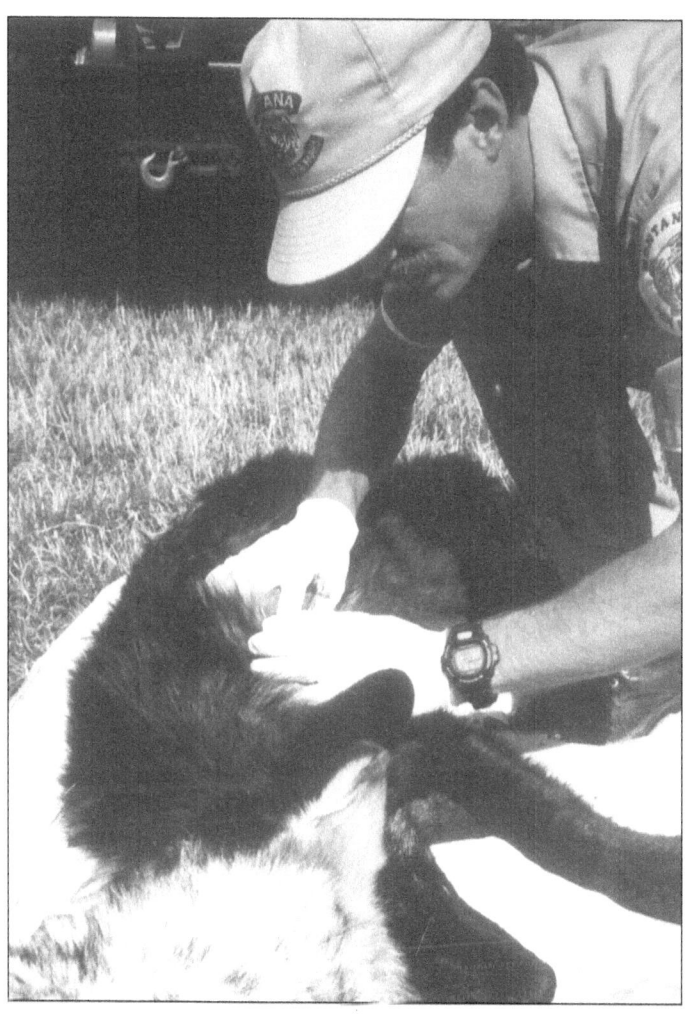

This captured wolf was one of two breeding females in the Sawtooth pack. Her collar had stopped functioning, so we replaced it. (Photo: Carter Niemeyer collection)

One of the captured Sawtooth pups with Haystack Butte in the backround. (Photo: Carter Niemeyer collection)

*A Sawtooth pup looks out from its metal crate.
(Photo courtesy Liz Bradley)*

*Delivering a captured Sawtooth adult.
Helicopter darting of wolves is done at no more than twenty to
forty feet above the animal and often in steep terrain.
The drugs used to capture and sedate wolves in 1996
were primarily telazol and ketamine.
(Photo courtesy Liz Bradley)*

Yellowstone National Park workers assemble wire panels for the wolves' one-acre pens. (Photo: National Park Service)

A Sawtooth pup walks the inside perimeter of its pen in Yellowstone.
(Photo: National Park Service)

An aerial view of an open wolf pen in Yellowstone.
(Photo: National Park Service)

Bob Cunningham and his mule team transport the Sawtooth pups for radio-collaring. Afterward, the pups would be delivered to the Nez Perce pen near Old Faithful. (Photo: National Park Service)

*Yellowstone's Doug Smith places radio collars on the
ten Sawtooth pups in early 1997.
This would be the first time the nearly year-old pups were collared,
and the day they officially became members of the park's Nez Perce pack.
(Photo: National Park Service)*

Wolf 27 is readied for a helicopter flight to the waiting ground crew near Dean, Montana. This was the first time I'd handled 27 since she had become a Yellowstone wolf. Drugs used to temporarily immobilize a wolf often cause the animal's tongue to hang out of its mouth.
(Photo: Carter Niemeyer collection)

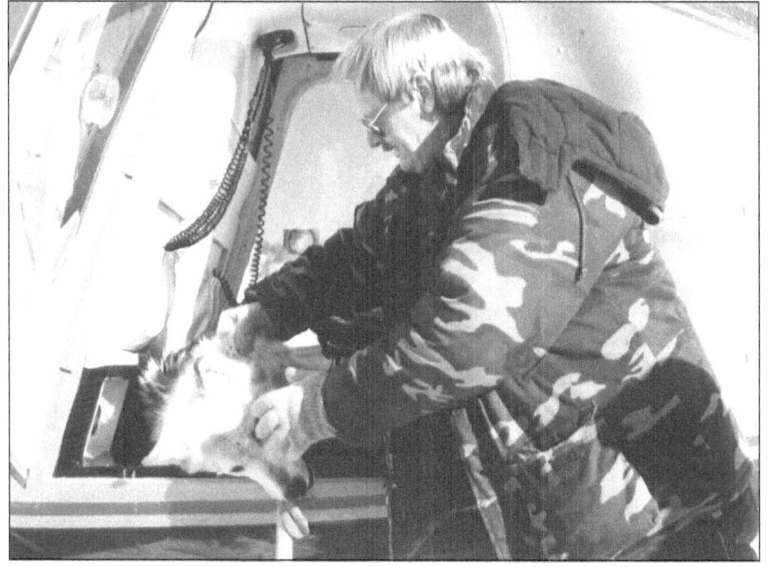

Once we put wolf 48 in Yellowstone National Park she stayed there. Capture teams often handle wolves by their neck scruffs, which are densely furred and have loose skin. "Scruffing" wolves is also for handler safety because it controls their heads.
(Photo: Carter Niemeyer collection)

Chapter 6
Four Pups

The Rocky Mountain Front is where mountains and prairie come together, a paragon of wildness and biological diversity. It's a place where grizzly bears—the tip-top of the food chain—can thrive. A place like this is more valuable to me than gold, and now wolves had come back on their own, completing the picture. Absent for more than fifty years, their howls once again filled the air, and an entire family of these iconic creatures was living on a massive ranch near Augusta Montana—and killing cattle.

Ranches and public lands kept development out and allowed wildlife to roam. However, most ranchers squeaked by financially, year to year. The wolf problem wasn't as simple as telling these folks to put up with the losses and the stress. If we wanted wolves to live here, and to repopulate their historic ranges, we couldn't let them eat livestock.

I had to straighten out this contradiction in my mind: wolves were neither good nor bad, they just *were*. Most of the trappers I worked with didn't share this feeling, nor did my supervisor. I knew the only way wolves could exist on this modern landscape was if they could put up with our harsh management approach. Troubling decisions lay ahead.

I worked alone in Montana, Idaho and Wyoming, driving hundreds of miles as a matter of routine, often late into the night. I sometimes examined livestock carcasses in the beam of my truck's headlights, or by headlamp. My job was to determine how the animals died and if wolves were to blame, to do something about it.

I rarely stayed in one place for more than a day or two. I mostly lived in my truck, ate on the road and washed my clothes when I could find a laundromat. Soon I was being asked to train other trappers in other states in case wolves showed up there. I was never home, so no surprise that I ended up divorced. I was married to my job. Few people involved in wolf reintroduction stayed happily married. Our work became our lives and tore our other relationships apart.

Even though I wasn't around the Sawtooth pack every day, their situation was always on my mind. I had a sinking feeling that these wolves would all end up dead, like so many of the early wolves. The ranchers were losing patience, and it was hard to blame them.

The capture plan sketched out for the Sawtooth pups would be the most ambitious one ever, outside of the Great Lakes region. In the upper Midwest, trappers couldn't use helicopters because of the dense vegetation, but most of the time in the wide-open West, a helicopter and a spotter plane were the tools of choice. Joe Fontaine and I smoothed out the scheduling wrinkles with pilots, biologists and fuel haulers. Bangs made more phone calls. The final detail we needed was permission from the landowners to make a commotion; the takeoffs, landings and low flights could be alarming for cattle and neighbors.

Finally, on August 29, 1996 everyone converged on the LF's airstrip. Ranch families joined the ground crew to watch the action.

Roger Stradley was our spotter pilot in his canary-yellow Super Cub. Roger had more than sixty thousand hours of backcountry flight time and for years had been the go-to guy for Yellowstone researchers who radio-tracked elk, mountain lions, grizzly bears, and now wolves. Bangs would ride with Stradley, flying high above the rest of us to locate the Sawtooth pack. I was the gunner, hanging out the right side of Gipe's chopper. Fontaine kept charge of the ground crew and waited for results. We communicated by two-way radio.

As the engines hummed on the airstrip, rancher JT Weisner and LF foreman Tim Tew pulled me aside.

"You'd be doing us all a big favor if you got rid of that black wolf. She's the problem." Weisner pushed back his hat. "Every time our cattle are being chased or something gets killed, we always see her."

He was talking about Bonnie. I asked about Clyde, the big male, the gray one. Weisner shook his head. "He never seems to be around." Tew nodded in agreement.

I relayed the message to Bangs.

"I gotta think about it," he said. "But take your shotgun with you."

It didn't take long for Stradley and Bangs to locate the wolves. Telemetry showed they were hanging around Haystack Butte, an odd land feature rising two thousand feet above the surrounding rangeland, visible for miles. In their journals, Lewis and Clark wrote about Haystack Butte, originally named Shishequaw.

The ground team trucked their equipment closer to the conical butte, pulling into a grassy meadow next to the county road. A half mile to the west, the wolf family lazed at the edge of a pasture that abutted forested foothills. But they quickly figured out the flying machines were after them. They leapt from their naps and took off toward the scattered pines, pups following the adults.

Stradley went higher so the chopper could go lower.

"Go ahead and kill that black female," Bangs' voice crackled over the radio. "Catch a different adult and we'll put a collar on it." I lifted my 12-gauge, pointed it out the doorless chopper, and chambered a round. I hated doing this, but whenever I put a shotgun in a helicopter there was a good chance I was going to have to use it. In the next moment, Bonnie was dead. I shot her again to make sure.

I switched to the dart gun and focused on a gray adult that was wearing a defunct collar. Gipe maneuvered the helicopter above the trees to keep the wolf from trying to run into the timber. When the wolf turned and dashed toward an open meadow, I got my chance. Gipe got me within twenty feet, and I fired.

"We got a hit!" I shouted.

Gipe banked away sharply to give the wolf some space, trying to avoid stressing it further. The animal made it to a ridgeline a half-mile away before it began to stumble, finally flopping down under tall pines. We circled a few times to be sure it wasn't going to jump up again, then Gipe landed us on a level spot some distance downhill.

This was another breeding female, which explained the numerous pups. She weakly licked her lips. Her eyes were open and her breathing shallow. Her heart rate was high. Late August was the worst time of year to be doing a high-speed capture. Too warm, and too much overhead canopy because the leaves were not yet falling. Seeing the wolves was difficult, which in turn made the chases longer.

I put a cover on her face to protect her eyes, gripped her by the scruff of her neck and started downslope towards the chopper, dragging her alongside me. I tried to avoid bumps and rocks and downed limbs. She was heavy, but wolves always seemed heavy when I had to move them by myself. I kept her head elevated to keep sticks and dirt out of her face and clutched at saplings as I made my way downslope. Normally I would have put her on my shoulders, but I didn't dare in this uneven footing. Gipe met me part way and helped. In the helicopter, he positioned her on my lap for the short flight to the ground crew.

At the trucks, the biologists took over. They measured her and monitored her heart rate and temperature, then hoisted her into a sling attached to a hanging scale and wrote down her weight: eighty pounds. The crew replaced the dead collar. Liz Bradley added a couple of lines to her diary:

> ....*Her feet were in poor condition; she was missing a few toes on one foot and another was swollen and calcified as if she had broken it before. Other than that, she was in good shape. She was released later in the day.*

More than a few of the Sawtooths had damaged toes, feet and legs. They were either being targeted or had been injured in traps meant for coyotes.

Stradley and Bangs were still in the air and had found the rest of the pack. The disappearance of their female leaders confused the pups. They hesitated instead of running. We moved in.

There were fourteen puppies as far as I could tell, gangly and clumsy at four and a half months old. They were about the size of large coyotes, some gray, some black. They looked like they each weighed about fifty pounds.

This capture was going to be a challenge. The pups lacked body mass and muscle, which meant it might be hard to dart them without injuring them. I switched to the weakest charges so the aluminum darts would stick in the youngsters and not go through them or make terrible wounds. Soon I was overthinking shots, worrying about wounding the pups.

Gipe quickly adjusted to my predicament and hovered as close to the wolves as he could. When the youngsters crossed openings in the forest canopy, I was ready. Soon four pups were down. We landed and retrieved two of them, and the ground crews jumped on ATVs and found the other two.

Bradley wrote:

> *Four pups were brought in: three gray females and a black male.*
>
> *They were all in excellent condition and weighed between 50-55 pounds. They were put in the carrying cages and readied for their trip to Yellowstone.*
>
> *We monitored their temperatures and cooled them off with cold water if they were too hot… They were very stressed when they woke up. Their dart wounds were treated with Betadine.*

We had spent the better part of three hours capturing the pups. Bangs called it a day. Gipe and I retrieved Bonnie and loaded her onto an outside tray. We returned to the LF for a debriefing and sent the pilots on their way.

Mark Downey, a reporter from the *Great Falls Tribune*, was waiting for a quote from Bangs. Downey asked about the decision to kill Bonnie and leave some of the pups behind.

"The idea is, we're not going to let them keep eating livestock. But we're going to leave them here," Bangs said.

The ground crew loaded the captured Sawtooth pups into a couple of heavy metal crates and started toward Yellowstone.

Later in the LF barn, I skinned Bonnie. Her scant fur was dull and sun-bleached, a typical summer wolf. Tew and Weisner watched my grim task in silence, our eyes meeting a few times. They weren't celebrating. They didn't hate wolves, but they'd found themselves in the middle of something they didn't ask for.

Bonnie's skull and pelt went into a freezer at the U.S. Fish and Wildlife Service's Helena office, then disappeared into the federal system. This was the case with dozens of wolf carcasses over the years. Pelts and skulls were show-and-tell items and were in big demand by universities, non-profits and government agencies as educational tools. I was a taxidermist and assigned myself the duty of boiling and cleaning the skulls of these early wild wolves, but I didn't have time to deal with the Sawtooths. I hoped whoever preserved Bonnie's skull would write her name on it. She was an historic animal.

As I headed home, I thought about the day. I wondered how people would react when they opened their morning newspapers.

Chapter 7
From Halfway to Nez Perce

The six wolves in Yellowstone's original Nez Perce pack came from a family of eight captured near the Halfway River in British Columbia. Two of the eight were deemed non-breeding adults and sent to Central Idaho with an assortment of other non-breeders.

In Yellowstone, the wolves were released into ten-foot-tall acclimation pens constructed of stiff wire fencing. Each pen was an acre in size and had a forty-five-degree interior overhang to discourage escapes. Each also had a buried wire apron along the bottom perimeter. An exterior electric fence kept bears and bison from intruding on these newcomers.

The enclosures all were located along creeks in the park so the wolves had a natural water source. Nez Perce Creek trickled through the Nez Perce pen north of Old Faithful. Like the other wolves transported from Canada in 1995, each Nez Perce wolf was radio-collared, ear-tagged and given an identification number.

This was the first time anyone had assigned numbers to wolves as a way to identify them. Originally, the Yellowstone wolves were known as R-2, R-3, etc. The R stood for red ear tags. In Idaho, the identifying numbers began with B for blue ear tags. The number stood for the order in which each animal was sorted and processed in Canada before being put on a plane to the United States.

Soon after reintroduction Yellowstone researchers dropped the R—and the red tags—because they didn't want their wolves to wear the unsightly and mostly unnecessary form of identification. On their data sheets researchers added another letter after each wolf's assigned number: M for male, F for female.

Much later, Yellowstone wolf historians outside the park tacked on a final letter for their own records: "g" for gray (or any variation of gray, including white), or "b" for black. The system created an alphabet soup of sorts, but it helped keep track of the growing wolf population.

We often joked that we should write "Fluffy" or some such name on the data sheets when we were handling a wolf during capture. A number seemed so impersonal, but it was the way with scientists, and still is. It's populations that matter, not individuals, or so they say. Try telling that to people who follow Yellowstone's wolves.

The Nez Perce pack consisted of a breeding pair, 27Fg and 28Mg, and their pups: 26Fg, 29Mg, 30Fg, and 37Fg. They were an all-gray pack, which was and still is unusual. The mother wolf, 27, was nearly white and as wild as they come. In Canada, as she was pursued from the air, she had lunged and snapped at the helicopter. She wasn't leaving her home without a fight.

On April 2, 1996, Doug Smith and Mike Phillips cut a hole in the fence that held the Nez Perce wolves. They were free to go. The wolves were wary of this change, but soon the females disappeared into the park, with 27 as their leader.

Yellowstone biologists, with the help of pilot Roger Stradley, monitored these wolves' whereabouts. Meanwhile, the two Nez Perce males weren't sure what to make of the hole and were hesitant to leave. The adult, 28, was the biggest wolf in the entire reintroduction at 130 pounds. He and his yearling son, 29, loitered inside the pen for three days after the females left, then trotted off. They traveled together for two weeks before parting ways.

Following their release, the Nez Perce wolves took off in every direction. Wolf 27 headed straight out of the park with her female pups, 26, 30, and 37. They trotted north through the Absaroka-Beartooth wilderness and into the valley at Fishtail, Montana, where Vern and Averill Keller raised sheep. Soon 27 was killing lambs, and we quickly found out why: She had given birth to five pups.

The sheep killings caused an uproar, and ranchers called a meeting at the fire station in nearby Nye. That evening Ed Bangs, Yellowstone Wolf Project Leader Mike Phillips and I learned in very specific terms what these good people thought of wolves and the feds who had brought them here.

At the time, I was also in a scuffle with my employer, Wildlife Services. My boss didn't like wolves and the political heat that came with them. As a result, he wanted to micromanage my decisions at every turn. At the Nye meeting, he and other Wildlife Services guys stood with their arms folded, smiling at the ass-chewing Bangs, Phillips, and I took. This was another bit of sabotage that had begun with the Sawtooth situation. I reacted to all of it much the way wolf 27 might have—get out of my face and leave me alone. As a result, I began each day wondering if I'd still have a job by day's end.

Bangs came to my rescue, because the situation was starting to affect wolf management outside Yellowstone. He was an expert at making a few phone calls to high-powered people and getting things fixed. I had good relationships with ranchers, and Bangs didn't want petty meddling to jeopardize that.

"Go get 27," Bangs said. "I'll deal with Wildlife Services."

Stradley, during one of his flights to find the missing white wolf, saw her with five pups trotting close behind. He radioed me with his news. I'd been in the area trying to pick up her signal and headed to his location.

Stradley had a plan.

As he flew over, he threw a roll of toilet paper out of the plane's window to mark the spot where he'd seen the wolves. The tissue streamed down into the trees. Now I had a place to start trapping.

The three female Nez Perce pups, 26, 30, and 37, were less pups than yearlings now. They had been traveling with their mother, but she had routinely left them to fend for themselves, probably because she now had five new mouths to feed.

Wolf 27 was wily and wary and stuck to the mountains, keeping out of sight. I tried and failed to catch her in the forbidding terrain. She refused to step in the traps I set for her. I did, however, catch two of her new pups. I turned them over to Yellowstone officials and they were tagged as males 46Mg and 47Mg. The other three pups had disappeared. Wolf 46, lost a leg as a result of this capture. He'd been caught in a trap I'd set for his mother and ended up living out his life in captivity.

Another Yellowstone wolf, 15Mb of the Soda butte pack, stepped in yet another trap meant for 27. I'd first met him in Canada and named him Carter's Hope. Like 27, he'd taken to hassling sheep at the Keller Ranch. In a weird twist of fate, Carter's Hope later mated with 26, one of the missing Nez Perce youngsters.

I'd spent a frustrating month in non-stop rain trying to trap 27, but she was having none of it. Doug Smith wanted her back in the park for genetic purposes, but she was nearly impossible to entice. Maybe later I'd have more luck. Other wolf problems in other places were demanding my attention.

By June, Nez Perce pack brother and sister, 29 and 37, had found each other on the vast landscape and teamed up to harass cattle north of Yellowstone. They were captured and put back in the park, this time in the now-empty Rose Creek pen a mile or so uphill from the Buffalo Ranch in Lamar Valley. Rose Creek was the easiest pen to get to, so it was often used to rehabilitate wandering wolves. The siblings were slated for release again in August 1996. Maybe this time they'd behave.

The drama created by the Nez Perce wolves unfolded only months before the Sawtooth situation had descended into chaos. Because they were about to be assigned new roles as surrogate parents, the August release of 29 and 37 had been put on hold. These wolves were only yearlings, but we thought maybe they would bond with the four Sawtooth pups. We wanted to give the pups a chance, some of them at least. The situation wasn't ideal, but maybe our plan might work.

In the Augusta meadows where the Sawtooth pups had frolicked, they were classified as fully endangered, but once they were delivered to Yellowstone National Park, they became "non-essential experimental" under the reintroduction guidelines of the Endangered Species Act.

Wolf advocates were insulted at the suggestion that reintroduced wolves were "non-essential," but these were just words. The entire Yellowstone experiment, while spelled out formally in mountains of paperwork, was not so set in stone on the ground. Inside Yellowstone, and outside its boundaries, we did whatever was needed to keep wolves alive and out of trouble. Their continued existence became personal to us. We weren't sure what would happen from one day to the next, but we were committed to making reintroduction work.

The latest issue was pretty simple: How would the four Sawtooth youngsters do with these two yearling Nez Perce wolves? Biologists who fed and monitored them kept out of sight as best they could and hoped the wolves would turn into a family. The six would spend the winter in the pen and be released in the spring of 1997.

We were certain we'd created enough mayhem in the Sawtooth pack that it would disrupt their cattle-killing behavior. Better yet, maybe they would leave Augusta's ranch country altogether.

But two weeks later, the Sawtooths struck again.

Chapter 8
A Silver Lining

In September 1996, I was summoned to the Krone Ranch, where I confirmed what Ray Krone already knew: wolves had killed one of his calves.

The Krones didn't intend to change their ranching practices; their place was too big for that. They owned and leased thousands of acres of rugged Augusta countryside. Changing their ranching practices would be expensive and problematic. Their large herds of cattle couldn't be corralled.

To gain weight and meet market goals, the cattle needed to graze unimpeded—and not be attacked by predators. Traditional grazing practices in the mountain West involve turning cattle loose in the spring, and rounding them up in the fall. Cowboys checked on the herds periodically during the day, but seldom at night—and most wolf attacks happen at night.

From a practical standpoint, no one had the means or resources to stop a pack of wolves from killing livestock.

We had two choices: move the wolves or kill them.

Once again, we were about to go after the Sawtooths.

The capture team reassembled at the LF Ranch airstrip, a huge convenience for taking off, landing and processing captured wolves. We all assumed our previous roles. Bangs would decide, once airborne, how many adults he wanted killed.

The ground crew would be using the same kennels as before—the ones used to ship the 1995 reintroduced wolves. Some of those wolves had broken their teeth on the metal bars while they awaited transport to the U.S. They chewed and torqued the aluminum, in one case breaking free while being transported in a horse trailer. We didn't have a lot of options. These were the only kennels we had. We hoped they'd hold together.

The Krones had reported seeing many wolves in their pastures since the last Sawtooth roundup. Some of us doubted this, but once in the air, we could see for ourselves at least a dozen. This capture event was going to be a circus. As we approached the pack, the wolves scampered like mice, running in all directions.

Bradley wrote in her diary:

> *They thought there were 5 pups left out there and they planned on removing at least 4 of these but once they got in the air, they realized there were 10 pups left……. Which means there must've been a double clutch litter this year which is very rare.*
>
> *So apparently both the alpha black female that was killed before and the female we recollared must have both had litters….*

Bradley's observation was accurate: multiple breeding females in one pack. It was the first time any of us had witnessed this behavior.

As we crested a ridge in the chopper, we encountered a grizzly bear wearing a radio collar and streamers in its ears. The startled bear ran downslope and pilot Gipe radioed the ground crew to watch out.

No doubt this two-year-old grizzly, known as Wade, and his brother Stan, were scavenging beef carcasses on the Krone ranch. The grizzlies had been relocated once, but were back. Madel's offer to move carcasses apparently had fallen on deaf ears.

Today, however, we were focused on wolves.

A few of the gangly pups ran toward the tall timber. Gipe raced after them, swinging us into shooting position. Gipe and I had flown together a lot, and I trusted him completely. This was dangerous stuff. I was so focused on the dodging, zigzagging, jackrabbit-like targets that I didn't know up from down.

I heard the plane radioing us about wolf locations, which changed every few seconds, but I was focused on my target. I fired, watching the tranquilizer dart sail in a slow arc. The brightly-colored yarn tails on each aluminum tube helped me track their paths. Some hit the bony pups, some bounced off and landed on the ground.

I re-loaded and anchored one part of my brain on the wolves and the other on hazards like tall trees and hillsides. Load, re-load, reposition, aim, shoot, land, take off, hover, search.

We stopped only to refuel and pee. I averaged three darts per wolf. We eventually delivered seven drugged pups to the waiting ground crew; six would be going to Yellowstone, the seventh was turned loose wearing a radio collar.

Bangs radioed my next task: kill the gray female we had re-collared only a couple weeks earlier and dart and collar another adult.

We were still hopeful that killing a few family members would stop the wolves' habit of killing cattle.

Meanwhile, the ground crew was getting nervous. They were about to run out of kennels, and the day had turned hot. The crew doused the pups with water to cool them. We needed to wrap this up. Bangs agreed. At the airstrip, he announced that if the depredations continued he would order the deaths of more Sawtooth wolves. We were done moving them, he said, and Yellowstone officials were not interested in hosting livestock-killing adults.

I skinned the gray female and put her skull in a cooler. Fontaine and the crew loaded the metal crates containing the six pups into the back of his truck. He then drove them more than two hundred miles to Yellowstone, bringing the total number of captured Sawtooth pups to ten.

I wasn't convinced we'd heard the last of the Sawtooths. We'd destroyed their family structure and terrorized all of them, but even that hadn't stopped their desire to kill cattle. No one has ever come up with a satisfactory answer to this problem. Maybe killing livestock is its own reward, so there's no reason to stop. The first order of business is survival, and the first order of survival is to eat.

It makes sense that wolves might zero in on slow and plump cattle and sheep, yet most wolves eat elk and deer and other wild prey and steer clear of anything having to do with people and livestock. The idea that we were teaching the Sawtooth wolves a lesson by killing and harassing them was absurd. Wolves never learn a thing by being punished days or weeks after depredations. They are not interested in the lessons we try to teach them.

I rarely took vacation, but when this latest capture was over, I was ready for some time off. I took six weeks, and while I was away, the remnant Sawtooth wolves killed another of Krone's calves. Bangs kept his word, and a Wildlife Services gunner flew in and killed two more adult wolves. At least four pups were left.

Eradicating the Sawtooth pack wasn't our goal—our aim was to stop livestock depredations. Depite the number of times we disrupted their lives, the Sawtooth wolves—however many there were—persisted in the Augusta area. For years afterward, a wolf was occasionally shot there for eating cattle. Without radio collars in the pack, however, there was no easy way to follow them, and the fates of those four pups remained a mystery.

If there was a silver lining to this gloomy cloud, it was that we had saved a good share of the Sawtooth youngsters. The ten sent to Yellowstone had another chance at life, so from our standpoint the operation was successful.

We will never know how the wolves felt about it.

Chapter 9
A New Pack

Circumstances in a wild animal's life can change fast, particularly the weather.

The winter of 1996-97 was one of the worst on record, especially in the harsh high country of Yellowstone National Park. Because of this, the new Nez Perce pack would have to stay in its pen.

Later we all wondered if this terrible winter disadvantaged these inexperienced wolves. Maybe this abnormal confinement and lack of adult wolves to teach the youngsters how and what to hunt was the reason they later tended to go after livestock.

In January 1997, Doug Smith asked me to revisit my attempt to pluck wolf 27 from her adventure outside the park. We needed to stop her habit of killing sheep at the Keller Ranch. She had disappeared into the mountains, but had recently re-emerged and started hunting in the farm fields near Dean, Montana. Once I discovered her in the open, capturing her was a short chase by helicopter.

True to her nature, 27 wasn't going down without a fight. She snarled and snapped at the helicopter the same way she had in Canada. Ed Bangs had wanted 27 shot, but agreed to let her have one more chance. I eventually put a dart in her hip, and soon she was in a crate and on her way back to Yellowstone.

Weeks later, to our surprise, one of the missing yearlings from 27's latest litter turned up at the Keller Ranch. When we zoomed in with the helicopter, the light-colored wolf ran frantically, carrying a sheep ribcage in her mouth. She eventually dropped her prize, but kept running. I darted her, then carried her on my lap in the helicopter to my waiting truck.

Once on the ground, I put her next to me in the passenger's seat to keep her warm. It was seven below zero outside, and I didn't want her freezing to death lying in the back of my truck. I could keep an eye on her here. I kept a syringe of ketamine handy in case she woke up before we got to the park.

No sooner had she been put in the acclimation pen than this wolf, now known as Nez Perce wolf 48Fg, climbed the fence and ran away, roaming greater Yellowstone ever after. She did exactly what we wanted all of the wolves to do: stay in the park with each other.

I sometimes felt I spent all of my time in a helicopter or setting traps because a lot was happening with wolves in other parts of Montana as well.

The Boulder wolves, west of Helena, had lives similar to the Sawtooths. Disrupted with captures and removals, these pups also were destined for surrogate parents. The Trego, Kalispell and Eureka wolves, also were causing problems with livestock. All were moved or killed. Two reintroduced Idaho wolves settled in the Big Hole area along the Idaho-Montana border and started killing cattle. They were captured and sent to a Yellowstone pen for a time-out.

Not many people were willing to try to catch all of these wayward wolves alive, or even knew how, but I did. I wanted to try, anyway. Week in and week out, I handed off darted wolves to waiting ground crews like we were on a production line. Where the animals were taken after I caught them, I often had no idea.

In the deep snow of February 1997, Phillips, Smith and a few volunteers used long-handled dip nets to run down, capture, and sedate the ten Sawtooth pups in the Rose Creek pen. A mule-drawn sled was there to receive them, and the drugged wolves were laid in a row on the open bed.

The mules were a bit jumpy about their passengers, but their frosty-bearded handler managed the team expertly while negotiating a bumpy and treacherous hill. The sleeping wolves jostled along unawares, each wearing eye covers.

All arrived a short time later at the park's Buffalo Ranch barn in Lamar Valley. This day the wolves would be given official Yellowstone identities. Their dark muzzles and lack of big neck ruffs betrayed them as youngsters, but the Sawtooth pups were almost yearlings now and finally big enough to wear radio collars.

Seven were gray, three were black. Six females and four males. While snow continued to fall in the silent valley, Smith fitted each wolf with a radio collar.

They would now be Nez Perce wolves: 63Fg, 64Fg, 65Fg, 66Mb, 67Fb, 68Fg, 69Mg, 70Mg, 71Fb and 72Mg.

From the Buffalo Ranch the newly collared wolves were trucked more than seventy miles to the original Nez Perce pen near Old Faithful and reunited with original Nez Perce wolves 27, 29 and 37. Wolf 28 was still on the missing list.

This area was home to a lot of bison, familiar prey to the Canadian contingent of this pack. Smith wanted the new Nez Perce wolves turned loose in this region because of the large herds.

But first, the weather needed to improve.

Ice and snow storms blanketed everything in impenetrable frozen layers. Most elk, deer and bison had left the area months earlier. Those that stayed too long were stranded, and died.

The wolves waited.

They were a pack of thirteen until just before their release, when Nez Perce siblings 29 and 37 produced a litter of four pups. This kind of incestuous bond was unusual, but not unheard of. In the case of wolf 29, breeding with relatives became his somewhat bizarre trademark.

One of the new pups died almost immediately. Now this hodgepodge Nez Perce pack numbered sixteen. Doug Smith decided that two separate releases of eight wolves each might be the best way to convince the wolves to stay in the park. Maybe keeping the adults in the pen would make the youngsters hang around.

The first release, in early April 1997, consisted of Sawtooth yearlings 63, 64, 65, 67, 68, 69, 71, and 72.

The second release, in mid-June, included the original Nez Perce wolves, 27, 29, 37, and their three eight-week-old pups, who were all male and all gray. The pups were too small to collar, and were not given ear tags or any sort of identification. Biologists figured they would stay with their parents, and that would be enough to keep track of them.

The June release also included the two remaining Sawtooth wolves, 66 and 70. Not long after, five of the of these young wolves were seen killing a winter-stressed bison. Everyone celebrated this event as a good omen.

But few things with wolves ever go smoothly. Soon the loosely-knit bunch broke up and wandered widely. Most of them left the park, which meant that soon my phone would be ringing.

Chapter 10
The Walkabout

Their extended time together in the pen had failed to create bonds among the mix of Sawtooth and Nez Perce wolves. Once they trotted out of telemetry range, biologists had no way of knowing their whereabouts.

Pilot Roger Stradley tried to find the animals during routine flights, soaring high above obstacles that were known to block radio collar signals. He was an expert at zeroing in on wolves, but even he lost the Nez Perce bunch, no sooner picking up a signal than it dropped off. We wondered if their collars had stopped working. Or maybe they were so far away they were simply gone.

Doug Smith shared his list of missing wolves with other agencies in hopes of one day finding the animals. We were confident most had fled Yellowstone. I kept a copy of the list in my truck and programmed the collar frequencies into my radio receiver, scanning continuously wherever I drove, hoping for that familiar pinging sound. But a wolf can easily travel hundreds of miles in a short time, and we really didn't know where these animals might end up.

Within three months of their release, four of the ten former Sawtooth wolves were dead at the hands of people: two shot, one hit by a car, and one poisoned by an M-44 sodium cyanide device designed to kill coyotes. The rest of the pack were still missing.

In May 1997, another monumental Yellowstone dispersal happened: Mike Phillips left the park to become executive director of the Turner Endangered Species Fund. Fortunately, Doug Smith stepped into Mike's shoes without missing a beat and would spend the next twenty-seven years immersed in Yellowstone wolf recovery. He, like Bangs, kept me on speed-dial. Soon he had a tip about some of his missing wolves.

"I've got a bunch on walkabout," Smith lamented to me on the phone in September. "See if you can bring them back."

The wolves needed to settle in somewhere before we could go after them. We discovered they had made their way northwest toward Cameron, Montana, crossing Highway 287 and the Madison River before entering the Madison-Wall Creek Wildlife Management Area. In the coming months this would be winter range for thousands of elk.

It was beautiful country, but the wolves didn't stay long. They continued west, into the Gravelly Range and Beaverhead-Deer Lodge National Forest.

Pilot Stradley had been keeping an eye on them and picked up their location near Dillon, Montana in a place called Sage Creek. The wolves seemed to like this area and were staying put. They killed two calves, maybe three.

Now, in addition to a missing wolf event, this was a depredation event.

I ordered up a helicopter and asked pilot Tim Graff if he was available. We'd chased down plenty of wildlife together. Graff said yes. By now it was October. I canceled my annual elk hunt and packed a bag.

The known escapees were 27, 29, 67, 70 and 72. Smith suspected the pups of 29 and 37 might be with the group as well.

All were likely following the white matriarch, 27, who was constantly on the move. She never seemed content since she'd been taken from her home in British Columbia. She was a confirmed sheep killer, and recently had killed two calves near Sage Creek. Ed Bangs had decided her time was up. Smith wanted 27 back in the park, but didn't challenge Bangs' decision to eliminate her.

With Graff's expert flying, I quickly darted a collared yearling, which turned out to be wolf 67. Then I put a dart in an uncollared gray.

Wolf 27 appeared next, but I balked. I was sick of killing wolves, and I really didn't want to kill 27. She was a survivor, and she just wanted to be left alone. Let someone else kill her, I said to myself. I'll put a dart in her and bring her in, but they can do the deed.

I took the shot, and the dart sailed toward 27, but instead of hitting her, it stuck solidly in her radio collar. She ducked into a stand of tall pines and disappeared.

I didn't have time to worry about her right then.

Stradley radioed that the two I'd already darted were down. The uncollared gray would become 92Mg. A lone coyote stood close to wolf 67, watching us. The coyote didn't seem frightened or even alarmed. What was it thinking, I wondered.

Just then a large radio-collared gray bolted from nearby sagebrush. Graff got me close, and I hit my target. This was wolf 29. We followed him, and he soon tipped over in the snow.

One by one, Graff picked landing sites and we lifted each wolf into the chopper, then headed for the ground crew. When we arrived, reporter Perry Backus helped unload the wolves and snapped a few photos for tomorrow's story in the *Montana Standard*.

Graff and I were soon airborne again. In the distance Stradley's plane circled high over the foothills. He radioed that he was watching two large grays trotting side by side. I leaned out the helicopter door and got ready as Graff slipped in behind the wolves. My first dart hit one in the hip.

"Go ahead and follow that one," Graff's voice crackled in my headset, instructing Stradley.

The yellow plane banked away to follow the drugged wolf, who had now separated from its pal. I put another dart in the chamber. When we overtook the second gray, I hit it too. These turned out to be Sawtooth brothers 70 and 72.

Now I turned my attention to the unfinished business with 27.

Following Stradley, we skimmed the treetops on a high ridge nearby. He had zeroed in on 27 with his receiver. No other wolves were around, at least none wearing collars that he could follow.

The signal pinged louder as he got closer to 27, but she remained hidden in the timber below. We landed in a clearing and walked among the trees, hoping to roust her. Stradley tried to do the same by buzzing the treetops.

"She just ran out and heading north!" Stradley radioed.

We hotfooted it back to the idling chopper.

Wolf 27 seemed to fly across the snow, almost invisible in her white coat. Then she suddenly stopped. A woven wire sheep fence blocked her way. She shoved her head into it, trying to force her way through. In the old days she would have lunged wildly at our helicopter, but now she was just frantic. I reached for my shotgun and ended her life.

As we slipped her into a body bag, Graff asked if I wanted a photo.

No. I didn't want to remember her this way.

Later, Doug Smith gave me 27's collar with the dart still in it. I hung the dirty, scuffed memento on the wall in my office—a reminder of a terrible day. I hoped I would never have to do something like this again. I still think about 27, and how she had no concept that she ever did anything wrong.

Graff radioed the ground crew that the chopper was nearly out of fuel, and we were returning to the Dillon airport. But just as we started back, Stradley's voice came over the radio.

"I found another radio-collared wolf on Blacktail Deer Creek. Do you want to come up here?"

Blacktail Deer Creek was about fifteen air miles away.

"You wanna give it a try?" Graff looked at me. He was serious.

"Are you sure we have enough fuel?" I tried not to sound worried.

"I think we can do it," he said.

We angled southeast, soon arriving at the confluence of Blacktail and Rock creeks. This was a location I knew well. In the 1970s I had trapped and moved hundreds of golden eagles in the area because they had been preying on domestic lambs.

Stradley soared above us, keeping tabs on the wolf. The only place for this one to hide was in the scattered patches of sagebrush. A quarter mile distant, I spotted a lone canine trotting along another woven wire fence, trying to find a way through.

This was a surprise. It was wolf 37, another of the original transplants from Canada. She wasn't on the roster of missing wolves. She was the sibling and mate of 29 and the mother of 92, both of whom I had just darted.

Like her white mother, 27, this wolf was in a panic, poking her head through the fence in hopes of escaping from the loud, hovering helicopter. Graff approached her slowly and I took an easy shot with my dart gun. Minutes later, she was lying in the back seat of the helicopter. I draped a bandana over her face for the short ride to the Dillon airport.

As we made a beeline toward fuel and the waiting ground crew, we encountered more than a thousand sheep that had been hidden from view below the rim of a hill. A herder was holding a gate open, while his dogs urged the animals along. Graff veered us away to avoid spooking the sheep. The herder looked up and waved. Wolf 37 had been caught less than a half-mile from the flock.

When we landed, the usually quiet airport was a bustle of activity. Trucks and cars filled the small parking lot, and a dozen people were standing around, some in Stetsons.

Smith's team offloaded 37, but I kept 27's body bag out of sight. Local sheepman Joe Helle stopped by with his sons to see the wolves.

His brother-in-law's flock was the one we had just flown over. These were the same men who were having trouble with golden eagles back in the '70s. I'd known Helle a long time. He was the former president of the Montana Woolgrowers Association and had massive influence over predator control in the state. How he found out we were capturing wolves that day was a mystery.

Two days later, I got a call from Helle. He had a story about wolf 37: she had been flirting with his sheep dogs when Stradley appeared and started circling. A few minutes later, we swooped in with the helicopter, causing the wolf to flee.

Helle laughed as he relayed the tale. His herder had watched the whole scene and was dumbfounded to see us catch the wolf and fly away with it.

Chapter 11
The Price of Being Wild

Within six months of their initial release in 1997, seven of the ten Sawtooth yearlings were dead. This unique experiment to save the pups and add to Yellowstone wolf genetics seemed destined for complete failure.

What else could go wrong, we wondered.

In addition to the pup disasters, wolf 29 had become an escape artist. He repeatedly attacked his wire pen, chipping and breaking his teeth. After the Dillon capture, he climbed his enclosure's ten-foot-tall fence using his claws and teeth. His sister/mate, 37, did the same and joined him on the outside.

Without a doubt, 29 was his late-mother's son—his mother being wolf 27. He was not going to let people control his life and seemed intent on helping all of his pack-mates escape incarceration. He dug furiously at the outside of the pen and freed the others. The group then started toward Dillon again. By the end of October, they were back within fifteen miles of where they had previously been caught.

I wondered if they were all following 37, who seemed hell-bent on getting back to that area as fast as she could, perhaps to see the guard dog she'd been flirting with.

I was on vacation when the second Dillon walkabout happened, so a gunner from Wildlife Services flew out just before Halloween, darted the six wolves and returned them once again to the Nez Perce pen in Yellowstone.

Two dead sheep belonging to the Helles were blamed on this most recent Nez Perce pack walkabout. The wolves had no sooner been returned to the pen than 29 and 37 climbed the fence and escaped yet again. How they were able to do this is astounding—especially 29, who had only nubs for teeth. A situation like 29's didn't mean a death sentence, though. A wolf's power is in the cooperation of the pack, and broken or missing canine teeth doesn't mean a wolf's jaws can't still crush its prey.

These wolves from the Halfway River of British Columbia were hardy and tenacious characters. It seemed to me, though, that we'd ruined their lives by capturing them, even if we didn't intend it to turn out that way.

The pair, 29 and 37, were free again, but they didn't stay together. At the park's edge, 29 stopped, turned around, and returned to the Nez Perce pen. He started digging at the edge of the fencing again to liberate the other captives, but this time the protective underground apron foiled his success, and he gave up.

With the approach of spring, 29 funneled his energy into courting his half-sister, wolf 48, who had escaped the pen on her own in early 1997. She had been content staying in the park, and 29 decided to stay there with her. He had a thing for his sisters. The pair produced one pup in a den a short distance from the Nez Perce enclosure.

Late in 1998, wolf 29 left Yellowstone for good. His travels took him not into more disasters with livestock, but south into

Wyoming's Grand Teton National Park, where he helped form one of its earliest wolf packs.

Wolf 37 also left Yellowstone again. She headed straight back to Dillon for the third time. She seemed to be looking for something, maybe her pups, 93 and 94, or maybe she was headed back to see her boyfriend, the sheep-dog. Whatever she was doing, she'd worn out her welcome in this livestock area, and in November 1997 she was shot by Wildlife Services.

At the start of 1998, the Nez Perce pack had been reduced to five animals: 48, 92, 67, 70 and 72. By summer, all had moved into Yellowstone's Madison River headwaters area, which was full of elk and bison.

Life was uneventful for a while, but with this pack, nothing stayed rosy for long.

In August, wolf 67 left abruptly, wandering livestock pastures near Lima, Montana. One morning a rancher saw a black, radio-collared wolf cornering one of his calves against a fence. Wildlife Services contacted Ed Bangs, who OK'd the killing of this former Sawtooth wolf. It was a situation that was not likely to improve.

Now only four Nez Perce wolves remained.

In the spring of 1999, males 70, 72, and 92, along with female 48, formed a new version of the Nez Perce pack. For the first time, this group started acting like a true family. They were the only pack that was entirely gray, which was unique because a gray coat color is a recessive trait.

Wolf 48 was especially light-colored, perhaps inheriting it from her mother, the nearly white warrior, 27. She may also have inherited a fiery temper and superb survival skills from mom.

Sawtooth brothers 70 and 72— known among local wolf-watchers by the misnomer, "Bad Boys of Choteau"—possessed personalities similar to 48, even though they were unrelated. The two brothers were always together. Always. They hunted and lived as if they were one animal. They looked identical.

After the Dillon captures, the four Nez Perce wolves settled down in Yellowstone and took up residency in the Madison-Firehole region, a locale that mirrored their personalities. They lived among the scorching geysers, hot springs and mud pots, and were among the first wolves to kill bison—not easy prey. Wolves 70 and 72 both appeared to be breeders, and 48 gave birth to five pups in early 1999. All survived in spite of a heavy spring snow.

Living in Yellowstone National Park seems like it would be heaven for wolves, but even this place can't guarantee a long life. Fights with other packs, extreme weather, dangerous prey and any number of hazards kill wolves regularly in this wild wonderland.

In January 2001, wolf 92 was found dead, possibly killed by another wolf along the Snake River where it exited the park. His brothers, 93 and 94, seemed to have vanished. Rumors flew that the two young wolves were left behind in Dillon after the first walkabout, and it was why their mother, 37, kept returning to that area. But biologists assumed 93 and 94 were traveling with the rest of the pack. The brothers were last seen in the northwest corner of Yellowstone in September 1997. No one could be absolutely sure about any of it. Neither had radio collars, so once they disappeared, their fates were unknown.

Not all of the park's wolves wore radio collars. This also was the case with Idaho's packs. It's not possible or necessary to collar all members of a pack; one or two is usually enough to keep track of a pack. Many people object to collaring, period. Maybe one day most of it will end, though probably not in the park. Yellowstone biologists have too much time and energy invested in ongoing research. Also, many people want to know all about Yellowstone's wolves. We can't seem to leave them alone. If we didn't collar them, we wouldn't know much about their lives. And for the Yellowstone wolves, it has been quite a story.

Doug Smith invited me to help capture wolves in the park in January 2000. It was the last time I touched a Sawtooth wolf. Number 72 needed his aging collar replaced. Our fixed-wing pilot was once more Roger Stradley in his yellow Super Cub.

Wolf 72 was a few months shy of his fourth birthday. He was magnificent in his heavy winter coat and tipped the scale at one hundred twenty pounds.

Alongside 72 ran his nearly-grown pup and I darted him as well. This youngster became Nez Perce wolf 191Mg, but he didn't last long. He left the park the following year, killed a calf, and was shot by Wildlife Services.

Park biologists think that 70 and 72 shared breeding activities with 48, which would be just like the brothers. She continued to produce pups until 2003, when 72 developed a case of wanderlust and left Yellowstone, getting as far as the Green River in Wyoming.

The following spring 72 returned to his Nez Perce family and stayed a short while before turning around and heading back to the Green River. This time he killed cattle and was shot by Wildlife Services. He was at least nine years old.

After 72 left, wolf 70 became the sole breeding male of the Nez Perce pack. He was just past his ninth birthday—just like his brother—when the fierce Mollie's pack killed him in June 2005.

Wolf 70 was the last survivor of the Sawtooth transplants, and the last of Yellowstone's reintroduced wolves, which numbered forty-one with the addition of the Sawtooth pups.

Six months later, wolf 48, died near Old Faithful, defending her territory in a skirmish with the Gibbon Meadows wolves. At nearly ten years old, she was the oldest known wolf in Yellowstone.

By 2000, the Nez Perce pack numbered twenty-two animals, second in size only to the Druid pack, which numbered twenty-seven.

But after their brief apex the Nez Perce wolves slowly diminished, and by 2006 had dwindled to none.

They had officially blinked out.

Epilogue

The life of a wild animal is short, especially that of a wolf. When you think about all the threats waiting to destroy this particular species, it's miraculous if a wolf ever gets old.

Some wolves live ten or twelve years, but that's not common. The average in Yellowstone is currently just shy of six years. Outside of Yellowstone a wolf can expect to live only two or three years. When the end comes, it is often swift and brutal, whatever the cause.

Reporters questioned Ed Bangs about the disproportionate number of Sawtooth wolves that had died within months of their transfer to Yellowstone. What were people to make of this impromptu addition of ten pups to the park? Bangs was never one to mince words. He summed it up for the *Jackson Hole News and Guide*: "In hindsight, the idea sucked. Children without a lot of parental supervision don't turn out that good."

Bangs was echoing what wolf scientists had warned us about during reintroduction: wolf packs aren't just a bunch of animals that travel together. They live in complex social units—families—and every member has a specific role. Without that structure, youngsters don't learn the right lessons. Our experiences with wolves have shown this is generally true. Bangs simply put it in the vernacular.

In 2004 in Hayden Valley, the old haunt of the Nez Perce pack, Yellowstone biologists spotted a white wolf with her mate and two pups. They were uncollared; no one had ever noticed them before.

They were soon known as the Hayden Valley pack. Everyone who saw them and knew the history of wolves in the park suspected the white wolf, soon to be known as 540Fg, was one of the pups born four years earlier to Nez Perce wolves 72 and 48.

If they live long enough, most wolves will turn some version of silver or white, similar to people. Scientists have only recently begun figuring out the genetic reason for this, but somewhere in the mix of Sawtooth and Nez Perce packs, white wolves emerged. They weren't born white, but were lighter than most and turned almost totally white at an early age.

Princeton University geneticist Bridgett vonHoldt says there's no certain way to tell why this happens, other than age. The genetics behind this phenomenon, she says, is a "hot mess" of possibilities.

One thing is certain, however: the Bad Boys of Choteau—Sawtooth wolves 70 and 72—contributed significantly to genetic diversity in the park. They may have been the only two Sawtooth wolves who accomplished this feat, but their contributions were essential. It was exactly what we had hoped for from the beginning.

Hayden Valley wolf 540 was not the first or only white wolf to be seen in Yellowstone over the years, but she was certainly a rarity.

In 2005 she gave birth to two pups, one of which became white fairly quickly, becoming known as the Canyon Alpha Female, or "White Lady." This young white female remained uncollared because Yellowstone officials figured that collaring her mate, 712Mb, would make following the White Lady fairly easy.

Both 540 and her mate were killed by the Mollie's pack in 2007, but the White Lady and 712 went on to produce many pups over the next ten years. At one point they were the oldest mated pair in Yellowstone.

With advancing age, however, comes loss of power and vitality and the White Lady began wandering, as old wolves do. She was inside the Yellowstone park boundary when she was shot. Hikers found her dying beside a road and called for help. Yellowstone biologists arrived and euthanized her. She was twelve years old—incredibly old for a wild wolf.

The white wolf lineage did not end there.

One of the White Lady's pups born in Hayden Valley in 2010 went on to establish the Wapiti Lake pack. Like her mother and grandmother, the Wapiti Alpha Female turned white with age. She is the wolf on the cover of this book. She disappeared in 2021 and is presumed to have died that year.

The Wapiti Lake pack lives on at this writing, however, and from this lineage we can expect to see more white wolves. The appearance of these living ghosts in Yellowstone is a reminder of the Sawtooth and Nez Perce stories.

It's easy to kill wolves when they cause problems for people. Preserving them is much harder. Ed Bangs could have easily ordered the deaths of the entire Sawtooth pack. Perhaps such a loss wouldn't have mattered on a population level. Scientists always talk about populations, not individuals. Populations are what matter. There will always be more wolves where those came from. That's the thinking, anyway.

Instead, Bangs decided to save the ten Sawtooth pups. Unfortunately, wolves are not grateful for our gifts and continue to act like, well, wolves. They are their own worst enemies, simply by doing what they do. We have created a world where large, far-ranging carnivores don't have much room to live. They are on a short leash with humans.

The Sawtooth pack, and for that matter the Nez Perce pack, may have been incorrigible, but we gave them a chance—for some, many chances.

We may never completely understand wolves and why they do what they do—or why they turn white. But maybe this doesn't matter. Maybe our job is simply to appreciate them during their fleeting lives.

It would be nice to live in the kind of world where all wolves can become old and white.

Maybe in my next life.

And maybe the rest of the wolves I have known will be there, too.

Epitaphs of the Sawtooth
and Nez Perce Wolves

The Benchmark wolf/the Sawtooth male/ "Clyde" (1988-1995)

This light-colored male wolf of many names was born in British Columbia to the Wigwam pack in 1988 and caught in a foothold trap as a puppy.

Because he was too small to wear a radio collar, he was ear-tagged and released. Researchers from the University of Montana studied the Wigwam pack, but eventually lost track of its members. In 1989, one of the Wigwam males showed up in the Bob Marshall Wilderness in 1989 and was called "the Benchmark wolf."

When the Benchmark wolf was captured and radio-collared in 1993 he was still wearing a fragment of the yellow ear-tag from his Wigwam days. He and a dark female wolf roamed near Augusta, Montana and became known as "the Sawtooth male" and "the Sawtooth female"—or the Sawtooth pack. They also were nicknamed "Bonnie and Clyde."

Clyde's collar either fell off or was chewed off by other pack mates. He disappeared in 1995 or 1996 and was presumed illegally killed.

Bonnie, his black mate, was never collared. I shot her in 1996 for killing cattle.

26Fg (1995-1998)

After her release from the Nez Perce pen, 26Fg wandered for a while before revisiting the Nez Perce acclimation pen, which then held Soda Butte wolf 15Mb, who was suspected of killing sheep at the Keller Ranch.

I had named wolf 15 "Carter's Hope" in Canada because he was the first wolf darted for reintroduction. While Carter's Hope was in the pen, Nez Perce wolf 26 flirted with him through the fence. After his release, Carter's Hope and wolf 26 left the park and eventually produced five pups in the DuNoir Valley near Dubois, Wyoming. They were named the Washakie pack, the state's first official wolf pack in modern history.

In October 1997, Carter's Hope (1995-1997) was shot by Wildlife Services for killing cattle, and the following summer wolf 26 was shot for the same reason. Their pups scattered. One was later hit by a car, and the others were never seen again.

27Fg (age unknown)

White wolf 27Fg was the breeding female of the Halfway pack captured in British Columbia and placed in the Nez Perce acclimation pen in Yellowstone in 1996.

After her intial release, she separated from other pack members, traveled north out of Yellowstone, and gave birth to five pups. She soon began killing sheep, even though her teeth were worn and broken—probably because she, like others, tried to chew through metal crates and acclimation pens. Wolf 27 was recaptured and placed once again into a Yellowstone pen.

After her second release, she led her pack out of Yellowstone into Montana, again into livestock country. I shot her on October 8, 1997.

She was the heaviest female wolf released into Yellowstone, weighing one hundred fifteen pounds.

28Mg (age unknown)

This breeding male of the Halfway pack in British Columbia was captured in 1996 for reintroduction and placed in the Nez Perce acclimation pen in Yellowstone.

He and wolf 27 bred inside the pen, but after their release never reunited. On January 28, 1997 his radio collar emitted a mortality signal (two pulses per second rather than one) near Three Forks, Montana. He had been illegally shot and thrown into the Madison River. The case was never solved.

Wolf 28 never killed livestock. He was the largest wolf of the Yellowstone reintroduction at 130 pounds.

29Mg (1995-2001?)

Wolf 29Mg was a pup in British Columbia's Halfway pack before being captured and placed in the Nez Perce pen in Yellowstone in 1996.

He was known for breeding with his female relatives, a sister (37Fg), half-sister (48Fg) and two nieces (137Fb and 129Fb). He eventually left Yellowstone and settled in the Grand Teton National Park area. He and his two nieces became known as the "Jackson Trio," later to be called the Gros Ventre pack.

Wolf 29, the relentless fence-climber, escaped his Yellowstone pen twice. He was last seen in 2001; his radio collar had failed the previous year.

The circumstances of his death are unknown.

30Fg (1995-1998)

After reintroduction and release from the Nez Perce pen, wolf 30Fg wandered widely before pairing with the Lone Star pack breeding male, 35Mb. The two formed the new Thorofare pack in remote southeast Yellowstone.

The pair produced six pups in 1997 and remained together as a pack until wolf 30 and one of her pups were killed in an avalanche on January 9, 1998. They might have been trying to escape a territorial dispute with the Soda Butte wolves, which also caused the death of her mate that same day.

Two of 30's surviving pups, 129Fb and 137Fb, stayed together that winter and spring and eventually met up with their Nez Perce uncle, wolf 29. The three settled near Jackson, Wyoming and became known as the "Jackson Trio." They later moved into Grand Teton National Park as the park's first wolf pack in modern history, the Gros Ventre pack.

37Fg (1995-1997)

Wolf 37Fg was a pup of Nez Perce wolf 27 and had a similarly ferocious personality. She and five other Nez Perce wolves traveled from Yellowstone to the Dillon, Montana area twice for unknown reasons. When wolf 37 returned to Dillon a third time, in November 1997, she was shot by Wildlife Services.

46Mg (1996-2003)

Wolf pup 46Mg was accidentally caught in a foothold trap and sustained a severe foot injury. His entire leg eventually was amputated by a veterinarian. He was placed in captivity in Minnesota, where he was named Tripod.

He lived seven more years, siring two litters of pups, before dying on November 21, 2003 from complications of West Nile virus.

Nez Perce wolf 27 was his mother.

47Mg (1996-1996)

Wolf pup 47Mg was struck and killed by a car near Madison Junction in Yellowstone National Park on September 21, 1996. He was not yet a year old.

He was a pup of Nez Perce wolf 27 and was born outside of Yellowstone. He was captured, placed in a Yellowstone acclimation pen and later released in hopes that he would stay in the park.

48Fg (1996-2005)

Wolf 48Fg played an essential role in establishing what biologists called the "true Nez Perce pack" in Yellowstone until her death on December 7, 2005.

She was one of the few wolves that stayed in the park once she was transferred there from her natal home near Fishtail, Montana. She contributed genetic diversity to Yellowstone's wolves by mating with Sawtooth males 70 and 72.

Wolf 48 died battling with the Gibbons Meadows pack in a territorial dispute.

She was the nearly-white offspring of Nez Perce wolf 27.

63Fg (1996-1997)

After her release from the acclimation pen, wolf 63Fg wandered near Yellowstone for six months and showed promise of staying out of trouble and contributing to wolf recovery. Then she entered private land north of the park and killed three sheep.

Park officials recaptured her and took her back to the Hayden Valley. Within one week 63 returned to the same ranch and killed another sheep.

She was shot by Wildlife Services October 26, 1997.

64Fg (1996-1997)

When a Sweetgrass County rancher near Greycliff, Montana checked on his flock of sheep, he encountered what he thought was a coyote attacking one of his lambs.

He drove a half mile back to his house to retrieve his rifle. When he returned, the canine was more than one hundred yards away walking through a patch of trees. The man fired a single shot and killed the animal.

The serial number on the collar matched that of Sawtooth yearling 64Fg. The wolf had been "in the act of" killing livestock, so the shooting was deemed legal under federal law.

She likely had traversed the Absaroka Beartooth Wilderness. She was killed approximately one hundred miles northeast of the Nez Perce pen on June 6, 1997, less than two months after her release.

65Fg (1996-1997?)

Sawtooth yearling 65Fg remained inside Yellowstone National Park for six months before disappearing in October 1997.

The date, location and cause of her death are unknown.

66Mb (1996-1997)

Wolf 66Mb was one of two Sawtooth yearlings released with the Nez Perce wolves in mid-June 1997. He roamed free for one month before being hit by a car on Yellowstone's Norris to Canyon Road on July 14, 1997.

He was 20 miles from the Nez Perce acclimation pen.

67Fb (1996-1998)

After being released from the Nez Perce acclimation pen in April 1997 with her siblings, 67Fb initially remained in Yellowstone.

Later she and her pen mates left the park, were captured near Dillon, Montana, and returned to their Yellowstone pen.

In August of 1998, wolf 67 again left Yellowstone and traveled to the Dillon area. She was shot by Wildlife Services for harassing cattle.

68Fg (1996-1997)

In August 1997 more than ninety dead ewes and lambs lay all along Tosi Creek on the edge of the Gros Ventre Wilderness in the Bridger Teton National Forest. A wolf was accused of these deaths, but when I investigated, I found that coyotes and grizzly bears also were responsible.

The herder who accompanied the sheep described seeing a "wolf-dog" approach the animals. He fired a shot over the canine's head to scare it away. A few days later I trapped this animal—a radio-collared wolf. A quick scan for missing collars identified the wolf as 68Fg, a Sawtooth yearling. I returned her to the park. I had caught her one hundred miles southeast of the Nez Perce pen.

Within two weeks of her release, 68 returned to the same area and was accused of killing at least fifteen more sheep. In addition to this transgression, 68 and the herder's Great Pyrenees guard dog had become friends, traveling and bedding together. A Wildlife Services gunner shot 68 in September 1997 because she had become a chronic livestock killer. The guard dog was euthanized.

Defenders of Wildlife paid the sheep owner nearly seven thousand dollars for the losses, the largest depredation claim up to that time.

69Mg (1996-1997)

On July 3, 1997 a rancher in the tiny town of Leadore, Idaho, was awakened by a commotion in the sheep corral near his house. He grabbed his rifle and walked out to investigate.

A large canine wearing a collar was standing over a half-grown lamb. The man fired and killed the canine, which turned out to be wolf 69Mg, one of the Sawtooth pups.

The man was exonerated from any wrongdoing by U.S. Fish and Wildlife Service law enforcement agents because the wolf was "in the act of" attacking the lamb. A wolf—probably this wolf—also was implicated in the death of a calf at a neighboring ranch.

Wolf 69 was more than one hundred miles due west of his Yellowstone pen.

71Fb (1996-1997)

Shortly after her release from the Nez Perce pen, 71Fb, a Sawtooth pup, set out on her own from Yellowstone on a westerly course. She disappeared into rugged national forest lands, ending up in the Ruby River watershed in Madison County, Montana where she dug up an M-44 sodium cyanide device that killed her.

She was seventy miles northwest of her Yellowstone pen.

The M-44 had been set in the ground the previous autumn by a federal Wildlife Services trapper to kill coyotes on livestock range. The trapper discovered 71's body when he visited the site on May 12, 1997.

70Mg (1996-2005)
72Mg (1996-2004)

By 1998, the inseparable and identical brothers, 70Mg and 72Mg, were the last of the Sawtooth wolves surviving in Yellowstone National Park.

No one is certain who started calling them the "Bad Boys from Choteau," but whoever it was got the town wrong; they were closer to Augusta.

The siblings formed a bond with 48Fg to create what biologists called the "true Nez Perce wolf pack."

This pack existed from 1998 until 2005, with 72 assuming the role of dominant male until he left Yellowstone in 2004. He traveled into Wyoming and was shot by Wildlife Services for killing a cow and calf at the sprawling Bar Cross Ranch near Cora.

Wolf 70 was the last Sawtooth wolf and the last of Yellowstone's forty-one reintroduced wolves. He had taken over as 48's mate until he was killed in a fight with the formidable Mollie's pack in June 2005.

92Mg (1997-2001)

One of three surviving pups born in the Nez Perce pen in April 1997 to Nez Perce siblings 37Fg and 29Mg, wolf 92 remained a long-time member of the pack.

He was captured near Dillon, Montana, along with other pack members on October 8, 1997 and given his first radio collar. Doug Smith said he had previously been able to keep track of 92 based on his coat color and because he always was in the company of his parents.

He died in January 2001 after fighting with other wolves in the southwest corner of Yellowstone.

93Mg (1997-?)

Wolf 93Mg was one of three surviving pups born to Nez Perce siblings 37Fg and 29Mg in the Nez Perce pen in 1997.

He was never radio-collared and was last seen in Yellowstone in September 1997.

94Mg (1997-?)

Wolf 94Mg was one of three surviving pups born to Nez Perce siblings 37Fg and 29Mg in the Nez Perce pen in 1997.

He was never radio-collared, and like his litter mate, wolf 93Mg, was last seen in Yellowstone in September 1997.

Acknowledgements

I'd like to extend a hearty thank you to the following people for taking time to answer questions, read manuscripts, and dig deep in their files and their memories regarding the Sawtooth pack:

Dan Stahler, Liz Bradley, Bridgett vonHoldt, Mike Madel, Graeme McDougal, Keith Aune, Ed Bangs, Doug Smith, Larry Davis, Joe Fontaine, Diane Boyd, Mike Jimenez, Misi Stine, Soraya Long, David Klinger, Miles Blumhardt, Julie Argyle, Dee Lane, Perry Backus, Pat Finnegan, Jim Halfpenny and Leo Leckie.

A toast to those who have passed on: Bob Ream, Roger Stradley, Tim Tew, Ron Gipe, Seth Diamond and Nick Evans.

I'm also grateful to all of the pilots that helped me safely catch the Sawtooth and Nez Perce wolves: Bob Hawkins, Doug Getz, Tim Graff and Ron Gipe.

And finally, I am indebted to my editors, Linwood Laughy and my wife, Jenny. Their tireless help turned my many diary notes into the book you are now holding.

WORKS REFERENCED AND SUGGESTED READING

Gipson, P. S., E. E. Bangs, T. N. Bailey, D. K. Boyd, H. D. Cluff, D. W. Smith, and M. D. Jimenez. 2002 Color patterns among wolves in western North America. Wildlife Society Bulletin 30: 821-830.

Halfpenny, James. 2012. Charting Yellowstone Wolves: A Record of Wolf Restoration. Gardiner, MT: A Naturalist's World.

Halfpenny, J.C., L. Leckie and S. Baron. 2022. Charting Yellowstone Wolves: 25th Anniversary, Second Edition 2022. Gardiner, MT: A Naturalist's World.

Halfpenny, J.C., 2025. www.wolfgenes.info

Landis, Robert K. Landis Wildlife Films. landiswf@wispwest.net

Leckie, Leo. 2025. www.wolftales.info

Niemeyer, C. Personal diaries. 1975—

Phillips, M.K, and D.W. Smith. 1997. Yellowstone Wolf Project: Biennial Report 1995 and 1996. National Park Service, Yellowstone Center for Resources, Yellowstone National Park, Wyoming, YCR-NR-97-4.

Smith, D.W. 1998. Yellowstone Wolf Project: Annual Report, 1997. National Park Service, Yellowstone Center for Resources, Yellowstone National Park, Wyoming, YCR-NR-98-2.

Smith, D.W., K.M. Murphy, and D.S. Guernsey. 1999. Yellowstone Wolf Project: Annual Report, 1998. National Park Service, Yellowstone Center for Resources, Yellowstone National Park, Wyoming, YCR-NR-99-1.

Smith, D.W., K.M. Murphy, and D.S. Guernsey. 2000. Yellowstone Wolf Project: Annual Report, 1999. National Park Service, Yellowstone Center for Resources, Yellowstone National Park, Wyoming, YCR-NR-2000-01.

Smith, D.W., K.M. Murphy, and D.S. Guernsey. 2001. Yellowstone Wolf Project: Annual Report, 2000. National Park Service, Yellowstone Center for Resources, Yellowstone National Park, Wyoming, YCR-NR-2001-02.

USFWS (U.S. Fish and Wildlife Service). 1987. Northern Rocky Mountain Wolf Recovery Plan. US Fish and Wildlife Service, Denver, Colorado. 119pp.

vonHoldt, B.M., DeCandia A.L., Cassidy K.A., Stahler, E.E., Sinsheimer, J.S., Smith, D.W., and Stahler, D.R. 2024. Patterns of reproduction and autozygosity distinguish the breeding from nonbreeding gray wolves of Yellowstone National Park. Journal of Heredity. 2024: 115(4): 327-338.

www.ingramcontent.com/pod-product-compliance
Lightning Source LLC
Chambersburg PA
CBHW030553080526
44585CB00012B/362